THE GREAT DAYS

THE GREAT DAYS

by

WALTER BONATTI

Translated by
GEOFFREY SUTTON

LONDON
VICTOR GOLLANCZ LTD
1974

ISBN 0 575 01815 1

Printed in Great Britain by
The Camelot Press Ltd, Southampton

To Reinhold Messner,
last youthful hope of the
great tradition of mountaineering

Contents

List of Illustrations

NOTE

Most of the photographs were taken by the author. A
few were supplied by the following photographers, to
whom the author and publisher extend their thanks:
Carlo Moriondo, Cosimo Zappelli, Mario De Biasi,
Giorgio Lotti, Philippe Letellier, the *Tribune* of Lausanne,
and an unidentified photographer from Zermatt.

FOREWORD

by Dino Buzzati*

A FEW YEARS ago, I was asked to introduce Walter
Bonatti, who was giving a lecture at Arzignano, in the
province of Veneto. The request was doubly flattering,
since on the one hand I considered Bonatti to be one of
the greatest mountaineers in the world, and on the other
it implied that Bonatti had a certain regard for my own
work. I declined, since I have always known myself to be
quite incapable of even the most modest forms of public
speaking. However, our mutual friends insisted so much
that finally I gave in. After all, I thought, it can only be
for a couple of minutes at the most, and I was clear
enough about Bonatti although we had only met once.

My ideas on the subject seemed so clear and precise
that I took the risk of improvising without setting down
in black and white, word for word, what I had to say.
This was the height of folly. As I stood up on the platform to say my piece, my mind suddenly became an
aching void. The clear, precise ideas were gone. With
immense effort and much stammering and halting, I
babbled forth three or four remarkably fatuous sentences
which ended in general embarrassment—mine, the

* _Translator's note:_ A famous Italian writer whose best-known
book was perhaps _Il Deserto dei Tartari_ ("The Gobi Desert"), one of
the finest Italian novels of this century.

public's, and that of Bonatti, who had obviously been expecting something rather less painful.

To rub salt in the wound, Walter Bonatti then took the floor himself. I think the audience must really have sweated trying not to laugh at the idea that a speaker so self-possessed, elegant and articulate should have been introduced by a "writer" in such miserable fashion. I feel in the same psychological situation today in writing an introduction, a preface, call it whatever you like, to Bonatti's latest book. Naturally I am somewhat less at a loss for words on paper than in public speaking, but I am aware of the presumption and basic pointlessness of the exercise. Quite apart from his fame as a mountaineer, Bonatti has absolutely no need of recommendations as an author.

Nevertheless, as an old and negligible mountaineer, approximately equivalent in standard to a weight-lifter's barbell, and also as an old journalist, I at least feel in a position to judge what seemed to me the finest and most important things in this book. They are as follows:

First of all, Bonatti's exemplary narrative style, which has the virtue, rare in mountaineering literature, of being absolutely devoid of rhetoric. Its dense rhythm and lack of superfluity are particularly effective in the account of the tragedy of the central pillar of Fresnay on Mont Blanc, a terrible experience which, as you may remember, gave rise to an unimaginably stupid series of polemics. Ignorant of such scenes as we are, we are able to visualize the various mountain faces attacked by the author, an achievement comparable to making us understand an abstract sculpture by mere verbal description. Indeed, the faces are abstract sculptures, only thousands of metres high.

Another of the book's merits is its sometimes almost brutal sincerity, which by definition does not exclude pride in cases where Bonatti wishes to bring out the historical significance of some achievement, as when he says: "Perhaps I may sound immodest, but in the interests of objectivity I must be clear."

His act of faith in the moral and spiritual values of mountaineering seems to me exemplary. This has always been an awkward, delicate, unending matter to discuss. The pundits have written veritable tracts on the subject. Bonatti defines the terms of the problem from a decidedly modern standpoint, absolutely divorced from "traditional morality with its martyrs and ancient warriors". Consciously or not, this standpoint is essentially a rebellion against the shortcomings of our technically minded society. With equal intelligence, and without resentment or the cry of sacrilege, he disposes of those lame, antiquated arguments about the fundamental uselessness of mountaineering which are always bandied about when some disaster occurs.

But what I would most of all like to draw attention to in this book, over and above the alternating pages that tell of battles on the highest and most ferocious walls in the Alps, is a beautiful, noble and consuming sentiment which was not present in Bonatti's earlier works. I mean the sentiment of farewell which crops up here and there in various circumstances, and to which he has had the courage to dedicate a whole chapter.

The author's retirement from mountaineering was not imposed by advancing years. He is still a man in his prime, gifted with great physical resources and a truly prodigious force of character. It was a premeditated action. "Bonatti has now ceased to be Bonatti the mountaineer." And probably he has put an end to his titanic exploits at the wisest time, when his star has reached its zenith and could rise no farther, when his legend—the term is not too strong—is at its brightest, without the mortification of the smallest shadow. It must have been a difficult and bitter decision, but he conceals his melancholy with the elegance of an aristocrat. He smiles and seems satisfied, as though he felt the weight of no regret. Certainly he has not said goodbye to contact with nature. On the contrary, he has taken to journeying through the remotest, strangest and most inaccessible regions in the world in order to report their marvels with pen and camera—an apparatus which, it must be admitted, is one of the finest of inventions. In this book he tells us two such fascinating traveller's tales.

How many memories, how much manly emotion, what *lacrimae rerum* are dissimulated with marvellous reserve between the lines of the pages which follow. From the deck of the ship that is bearing him who knows where, towards who knows what amazing adventures perhaps as dangerous as the slanting, slippery holds of the north face of the Matterhorn, Bonatti seems to gaze at us with strangely shining eyes—has he not just told us that he was sure to be happy?—and we are all struck by an unexpected thought which it would perhaps be cruel to express here.

THE GREAT DAYS

I

The Great Tragedy

AMID THE SUBDUED murmur of the group by my bed-side, I recognized the voice of Dr Bassi.

"Incredible. With an azotemia like that, he should be dead."

His comment left me unmoved. I did not even care about the state of my hands, gashed by the rock and dis-coloured by frostbite, or my swollen, burning eyes. In one arm there was a needle, through which fluid was being slowly fed into my starved veins. If my state was certainly not comforting, it nevertheless felt like a re-birth compared with what it had been a few hours pre-viously. The bed was warm and dry to a degree beyond anything I could have hoped. As I lay motionless in its cozy depths I could feel the bones in my body starting to knit together as though they had been shattered.

So the hours went by. The drip from the serum bottle ceased. Around me all was quiet and calm at last, but nightmare images of precipices, blizzard, lightning, faces, despair and death continued to whirl through my mind. I set about recomposing the painful sequence of events.

By pure chance two parties—one consisting of the French climbers Pierre Mazeaud, Pierre Kohlmann,

Robert Guillaume and Antoine Vieille; the other of
Andrea Oggioni, Roberto Gallieni and myself—had
decided to attack the still unclimbed central pillar of
Fresnay on Mont Blanc the same day, Monday, 10 July
1961. It was a problem of outstanding mountaineering
interest owing to the striking beauty of the red granite
structure, its high altitude, the complicated and exhausting approach march, its severe isolation and,
naturally, the great technical difficulty of the climbing.
We had run into each other in the course of the approach,
and although momentarily disconcerted we had immediately decided to join forces in the name of that
open-hearted comradeship which knows neither frontiers
nor discrimination. The others were rated among the
best French climbers of the day, and for our part we
were considered to have a good knowledge of Mont
Blanc. The weather was fine and the barometric pressure
stood high.

Having tied together in three parties and taking turns
at leading, we reached a point only 80 metres below the
end of the difficulties in a mere day and a half from
Courmayeur. At this juncture, about noon on 11 July,
began perhaps the most unimaginable tragedy ever to
strike a party of trained and experienced mountaineers
on Mont Blanc.

As we made haste to reach the final vertical step we
noticed streamers of cloud beginning to form around us,
but since the goal was now so close we did not worry
particularly. "If there is going to be a storm, we shall
reach the summit before it," we said. An hour later,
however, after some 40 metres of overhanging climbing,

we were struck by a thunderstorm while at grips with the last difficulties. Leaving pitons, karabiners and étriers in place, we slid quickly back down the rope. As we reached the few narrow ledges at the tip of the 15 metre pinnacle we had nicknamed "the candle", a kind of buttress to the final overhangs, a violent blizzard set in.

Thunder and lightning burst around us; the air was saturated with electricity. The wind lashed our faces with blinding snow. We stood at over 4,500 metres on the tip of a pillar which is the lightning conductor of Mont Blanc. We three Italians settled down on a small ledge. The French were sorting themselves into two groups when without any warning a flash struck right beside Kohlmann's face. Under the force of the blow he reeled and had already overbalanced when with a bound Mazeaud grabbed him and succeeded in holding on. For several minutes he remained paralyzed as we hurriedly searched for coramine which Mazeaud then forced down his throat. At last his senses returned and we were able to finish arranging ourselves as the storm raged on. Oggioni, Gallieni and I were huddled together on one small ledge; Vieille, Guillaume and Mazeaud were on another to one side; and on another slightly more spacious one just below us lay Kohlmann by himself so that he could stretch out more comfortably. We had no way of knowing it at the time, but this may have been the beginning of his psychological drama.

Between us and the easy snow-ridge which led to the summit of Mont Blanc rose a mere 80 metres of unknown monolith. Beyond the summit lay not only victory but the safety of the Vallot hut and an easy descent towards

Chamonix. We needed a bare half-day of clearer weather to bring the adventure to a happy issue, but we were never to get it.

As darkness fell the storm grew still more violent. Closed in our bivouac sack, we could only judge it by the sound. When the thunder seemed to grow more distant our spirits would rise, only to be dashed as it returned again. The flashes dazzled us through the opaque fabric. Still full of life, we were absolutely powerless against the fury of the elements. All around us, attached to the same pitons as ourselves, hung the pitons, crampons and ice-axes needed for the climb. No better means of attracting lightning could be invented. We longed to hurl them away, but if we did that, how would we get up or down? Nobody spoke; we had all withdrawn into our own thoughts.

While we crouched there reflecting for the umpteenth time that our fate was in the lap of the gods, we suddenly felt an alien force convulse our legs, and a wild yell was torn from all our throats. A discharge of lightning had flowed over us. We had survived, but henceforward we all had the conviction that we might be incinerated at any moment. We called to one another, to be sure everyone was still there. There followed a terrifying stillness. We knew that the electrical charge was building up and must inevitably explode over us again. And indeed, a few minutes later, the shock was repeated even more violently, almost jerking us away from the face. Amid the united scream I clearly heard a voice saying: "We've got to get out of here!" but whether it was Oggioni's or Gallieni's I did not know. Prompted by desperation, these words reflected everybody's feelings. I was sure that it was all up with us, and believe that the others all thought the same. I looked back over the course of my life, summoning to mind beloved faces and other things that I should certainly not see again. These impressions occupied only a few instants, yet they were absolutely clear and seemed to last an incredibly long time.

Miraculously, the thunderstorm seemed to move away. The only sound was the pattering of the frozen snow on the rubberized fabric that covered us. We remained motionless. It was already dark, and no one bothered to look outside. Nobody spoke or ate; we were indifferent to what might happen. Although the falling snow was an extremely serious matter, it almost comforted us. We had escaped the lightning and we were alive. I had never known such a storm on a mountain face. No technique or ability could save a man from it.

Cramped up awkwardly in our bivouac sack for many hours, we began to feel the lack of oxygen. We therefore ripped a hole in the fabric, avidly inhaling the fresh air that flowed in. The sack was practically buried in snow, and the warmth of our breath formed a densely humid atmosphere inside it that, according to the changes in temperature outside, froze into ice crystals or melted into drops of water. I felt a reluctance to look at my watch so as not to be disappointed by the slowness of the passing of time. There was no conversation, merely grumbles about the cold, about the jeopardy we were in, or about the tormenting feeling of suffocation from which we all suffered. We had no idea how the French were getting on, but from time to time similar complaints drifted across to us from their ledge. At last the night stole by and a milky light heralded the dawn of Wednesday. Only then did we emerge from under our shelter, to be immediately staggered by the amount of snow that had fallen during the night. The French were completely submerged in it. On his narrow ledge below, Kohlmann had already risen to his feet and stood out as a dark form against the blazing horizon which gave promise of a splendid day. A feeling of happiness ran through us. The huge quantity of fresh-fallen snow and the terrible frost that had succeeded it were portents of fine weather. In a matter of moments we were all out of our sleeping-bags and ready to attack the last few pitches. I snapped a few photographs, which tragically were to prove the last, then we started to pack up the tent. While we were in the process of doing this the clouds suddenly formed again out of nowhere and we were struck by a violent squall. A pall of fresh snow came whirling up on the wind so that we could not tell whether it was snowing again or whether the gale was whipping up what had already fallen. Once more we pulled the tent-sack over our heads while the French did the same with their polythene sheet. This time Oggioni, Gallieni and I climbed down and settled ourselves on Kohlmann's slightly roomier and more comfortable ledge, while Kohlmann scrambled up three or four metres to where we had passed the night, taking with him his bivouac outfit consisting of a down-filled sleeping-bag and a plastic sheet in which he wrapped himself like a mummy. After anchoring himself to the piton we had left, he settled down again to wait like the rest of us.

During the clearing a few minutes earlier I had noted that the snow had fallen to a very low altitude, right down on to the green pastures of the lower hills. It seemed difficult to believe that the blizzard could begin again after so much snow had fallen. The French asked me what I thought it best to do. Still hoping that we should be able to reach the summit, the shortest road to safety, I proposed waiting. We had plenty of food and equipment and could therefore afford to hold on. At this time of the year bad weather never lasted long, and the very idea of climbing back down the pillar and the Fresnay glacier, so complicated and full of danger in blizzard conditions that it could not take less than a couple of days even though it was the simplest way, was thoroughly scarifying. Moreover, from the point we had already reached, half a day would see us to the summit.

Mazeaud and his companions were on a ledge anchored to a piton about six or seven metres away from me, with Kohlmann to one side. Mazeaud had a certain moral authority over the others, and he now suggested that as soon as the weather made it possible we two should peg our way up those tremendous, overhanging 80 metres, then bring up the others. The plan was agreed to, but the clearing never came. We swallowed bits of ham, meat and jam, but were unable to wash them down because the blizzard made it impossible to light the alcohol stove so as to melt snow.

It continued to snow. Nothing changed from hour to hour. From among the thoughts that crowded through my mind I tried to recall the details of similar situations when I had been cut off by bad weather in the mountains. At this time of year the storm had never lasted for more than one or two days at a time. I therefore thought to myself that as this one had already been going on for a whole day it could scarcely last more than another 24 hours. It was just a question of sitting it out, then we could move on.

Sitting it out in this cramped position, however, became more and more intolerable. We were jammed up against one another in a space barely adequate for one person. It was impossible to raise our heads or lean to one side, so that through being stuck in a bowed position it felt as though our spinal columns were about to split. In such circumstances it is easy to become irritable. At times the temptation to thrust aside the imprisoning envelope was strong, but woe to us if we did so. The three of us chatted of this and that, memories, projects, hopes, friendships, happy themes and troubled ones, to while away the time. Oggioni reminded me:

"Walter, do you remember how a month ago in Peru we said: 'One of these days we'll get to grips with that pillar'?"

His tone was ironic, because at the time we had thought that on our home mountains everything would be simpler, yet now we found ourselves in the same circumstances as on Nevado Rondoy, in far-off Peru, which we had been forced to climb through two days and two nights in blizzard conditions without any shelter. As for Gallieni, he was busy passing around vitamin pills to everybody, especially vitamins A and C. He even sent them up to the French by means of a rudimentary cableway rigged up with some nylon rope, and since they were a bit short of food he added some for good measure.

The need to urinate began to make itself felt. There could be no question of going outside the tent-sack. Oggioni and I therefore suggested to Gallieni that he should sacrifice his crash-helmet, which happened to be unlined. We used it in turn. It was a fearful performance. In order not to fall off in the process we had to hold on to each other and adopt the most contorted positions. Our many layers of clothing were a redoubtable obstacle, and in addition our feet were hanging over the edge into space. The operation took over half an hour.

By the time it was all over it was Wednesday evening. It was snowing harder than ever. Gallieni was nearest the edge, so I asked him which direction the wind was coming from. "Still out of the west," he replied. That meant continuing storm.

Mazeaud shouted down exuberantly: "As soon as it clears, you and I can start up. If you think it'll go more easily over to the left, we'll try there."

Oggioni, who could not understand French, asked me what he had said. I translated for him, and he agreed. The idea of getting moving seemed to cheer him. Mazeaud called back:

"Do you think we could start climbing even before it clears up completely?"

He knew well enough that from the summit of Mont Blanc I could find the way down in any conditions, as I had demonstrated on other occasions. I replied that I thought we could, but that we should wait for the night to go by. In my heart I felt practically certain that by the following morning the storm would be over.

Inside the sack our breath formed a saturated vapour that soaked us to the skin. I was worried by the thought of the intense cold that would precede the fine weather, and hoped I would be able to withstand it. If we came through that, we would be able to spend a few hours toasting ourselves in the warm sunlight before climbing the last step.

The night took us almost by surprise. We were too excited to sleep. Gallieni talked about his children. As for me, I was 3,000 metres lower down in the intimacy of my house with those I loved. Oggioni spoke of Portofino, where he had never been. "We climbers are a bunch of fools," he said. "With all the beautiful things there are in the world, we go and get stuck in situations like this." Gallieni replied: "And to think that in Milano Marittima I have a comfortable house, with the sea in front of it so calm and warm and shallow that you don't even need to swim if you don't feel like it. You can just walk for kilometres and kilometres." Oggioni covered up his anxiety with jokes. To all outward appearances he was the most undisturbed of the lot of us, but I knew that he and I were the only ones who realized the full extent of our desperate plight.

So the night of Wednesday to Thursday went by. As day dawned, Mazeaud came down to join us in our sack. The plastic sheet covering his sleeping-bag had been torn apart by the wind. Somehow we managed to contort ourselves so as to make room for him, and we spent the day trying to keep up our courage by telling each other that it was bound to be fine on Friday, although in our hearts none of us was convinced. Inwardly I was working out the safest way of beating a retreat back down the way we had come. It was clear to me that there was no more hope of reaching the top of the pillar on this occasion, although I did not say so to the others in order not to discourage them.

Mazeaud spoke to me about his ascent of my climb on the Dru, which he had done a week earlier. We promised each other to meet at Courmayeur or Chamonix in order to commemorate the ordeal we were now experiencing. All of us were suffering badly from thirst, which we tried to quench by crushing up little balls of snow to nibble and suck. I thought of the beauty of a simple household tap: all you had to do was turn it and water would go on coming out as long as you wanted. It was paradoxical to suffer so much from thirst in the midst of so much snow. Yet the mouth burned and chapped at the touch of the snow's cold fire.

Thus Thursday went by and another night thickened around us. During those long hours of darkness Oggioni and I, who were the most involved in the depths of the sack, suffered acutely from the lack of air. To him alone I whispered my intention to go down at any cost. Though horrified at the idea, he agreed. Slowly, slowly the night crept by. I had set my alarm for half-past three, and as it went off I called out to everybody:

"We've got to get out of here. If we sit around any longer it's going to be too late. We'll not have the strength left to get down."

The day began to dawn. It was now Friday morning, and the storm had not abated at all during the last 60 hours. Visibility was nil. Cloud and snow formed a grey, impenetrable amalgam. We decided to leave some of the kit behind. I had no ice-axe; somebody had knocked it off a ledge by mistake on the first day. We allocated the responsibilities for the descent. I was to go first, placing the pitons and the rappels. Mazeaud was to follow, with the job of helping in every way possible. Then came the others, with Oggioni, the rope-handling expert, bringing up the rear.

Precisely at 6 a.m. I set off into the whirling void, virtually blind, without any idea where I might fetch up. It was like being at sea in a squall. The spinning snow-eddies almost made me dizzy. My freedom of movement was hindered by the heavy sack and the ballast of pitons that I carried at my waist so as to construct a way of descent for the others. In order to find my way I had to scrutinize every feature of the rock, trying to remember each fold and wrinkle. Quite soon my eyes began to hurt with the strain of constantly staring into the stinging whiteness of the storm. Every manœuvre seemed un-ending, and the recovery of the rope each time to begin another abseil lasted an eternity. At times four or five of us were hanging from a single piton. I was obliged to work with bare hands. I had hardly arrived at one ledge, and for lack of any possibility of protection had craned outwards in balance to place the next piton, when I saw a shadow whizzing down the rope. It was Kohlmann, who had lost his grip on account of the cold and can-noned into me, projecting me into space. I shot off the edge, grabbing the half-hammered piton and swinging from it with all my weight.

About half-way down the pillar I reached the end of the rope without finding anywhere for the next stance or belay. Not even the tiniest ledge was to be seen, and the snow was adhering even to the underside of overhangs. Amid the shrieking of the gale I finally managed to convey to those above that I needed another rope to attach to the one from which I was suspended. After weighting it, they sent it down, and by means of some complicated acrobatics I succeeded in knotting it on and in starting off down again like a spider on a thread. By this time it had become impossible to speak with anybody. Dangling completely clear of the rock, I sought in vain for somewhere to anchor the rope. Either because I did not know where to stop, or on account of the enormous overhang which cut off all possibility of communication with the others who somewhere far above were waiting for a signal, I felt agitated and disturbed. Finally, after a series of bold swinging movements in empty space, I succeeded in reaching a projection of rock, from which I bellowed up through the blizzard to the others that they could come on. Presently the rope began to move up, and I took it that somebody was preparing to descend. Unexpectedly, however, it disappeared from sight, and I was left marooned on my jut of rock in the midst of the pillar with no way of getting down, wondering whether my companions had understood me or whether they would descend in another direction. I yelled at the top of my voice to show where I was. Seemingly endless minutes of anxiety went by, then a dark shape began to take form above me. It was Mazeaud, who had guessed the right direction.

We only succeeded in pulling down part of the long series of knotted ropes used in this unusual abseil, the rest remaining dramatically abandoned on the face. From this time on, we had only a limited amount of rope available. The descent continued with unvarying rhythm, each abseil producing some trying event. Nevertheless, we were gradually getting closer to the foot of the pillar. Our clothing was frozen to a shell of ice on the outside and saturated underneath.

The muffled blast of an avalanche showed me that we were nearly at the end of the pillar. It was late afternoon, and it seemed obvious that we should have to bivouac on the Col de Peuterey. On the flatter ground beyond the bergschrund the snow was extraordinarily deep, sometimes reaching right up to our chests. I sent Mazeaud ahead, followed by all the others, while I belayed and kept them on course. Presently they seemed to get bogged down in a mountainous snowdrift, so I moved through into the lead. Working by intuition, I ploughed on towards the best bivouac site. Although I could not see it, it was as though I had a photograph in my head. Behind me came Oggioni, and as we struggled forward we discussed the relative merits of sheltering in a crevasse and building an igloo, given that the snow was floury and loose. This was not so much for our benefit as for that of the French, who had no bivouac sack. With Mazeaud's approbation we opted for the crevasse.

Before Friday night fell we were all settled into our bivouac after twelve hours of abseiling. The most exhausted of us was apparently Kohlmann, so we put him into our tent-sack. With what remained of a gas cylinder

Oggioni (foreground) and Mazeaud are recognizable through the cloud at the base of the final overhang on the central pillar of Fresnay.

Ice-encrusted étriers and ropes on the final tower of the central pillar of Fresnay after the first night of storm. They were left on the face.

Guillaume made some hot tea and fed it to him. The cold was terrible. The wind never stopped blowing for an instant, whirling up tornadoes of snow more and more tormentingly throughout the night. We divided up the remaining food, prunes, chocolate, sugar and a bit of meat frozen stiff with the cold. Kohlmann showed me his fingers; they had turned livid. So that he could massage them back to life I passed him our flask of cooking alcohol, which was still almost full, but thoughtlessly he set it to his lips and began to swallow down the contents, which he perhaps mistook for some kind of liquor. Quickly I knocked it out of his hand, but not before he had taken a couple of gulps. Was he beginning to go mad?

The darkness was impenetrable. Our bivouac was an inferno of groans and shivering, the shrieking of the gale and snow which fell ever more thickly. Every so often we had to shake the tent clear of the heavy load that piled up on it. Each time I tried to light our spirit cooker the flame went out for lack of oxygen. To quench our thirst we were therefore obliged to eat snow as we had been doing for the last few days. Our position was desperate, but no one spoke of it. "Let's make a promise," suggested Oggioni. "If we get out of this alive, we'll forget that the pillar even exists." I gave my assent.

In the blizzard the night went by with desperate slowness. At 3.30 a.m. on Saturday morning, the same time as on the previous day, my alarm watch went off, rousing us from our cheerless resting places. We wanted to save time and get ourselves out of this terrifying and seemingly unending situation. Another 60 centimetres of

C

snow had fallen during the night. Nevertheless it seemed as though everyone had stood up well to the fourth atrocious bivouac, and we set off into the blizzard. I saw no point in discussing the situation with the others, who were now just following me blindly. Their trust made me feel the weight of my responsibility to lead them all back to safety via the only possible route, the dangerous Rochers Grüber. If we did not reach the Gamba hut by that evening, it would almost certainly be the end of us.

Before leaving, Guillaume gave Kohlmann an injection of coramine. In the meantime I had begun to plough a trench through the bottomless snow. We had roped up as a single party with myself in the lead, followed by Oggioni, then Gallieni, Mazeaud, Kohlmann, Vieille and Guillaume. The slopes we had to cross to reach the Rochers Grüber were frighteningly laden with fresh snow which was ready to slide away in an avalanche at any moment. I called out to the others to come across to me as quickly as possible and take up a safe position so that they could hold me on the rope in case I was swept away by an avalanche while making the track. In the event, I got across without incident, then shouted to the others to come on one at a time. When Vieille's turn came, however, he was unable to manage it, continually falling and struggling to his feet again. Guillaume, who was just behind, helped off his sack and left it on the slope, pushing him along. Nevertheless, Vieille seemed not to hear our calls. In the meantime, I set off down the first of the long series of rappels down the Rochers Grüber. The sky was looking less stormy, but the respite was to be brief. I could hear the others encouraging Vieille, who still had not made the traverse. I bellowed up to them to hurry. Meanwhile Kohlmann had abseiled down to join me. Half an hour went by. Gallieni informed me that Vieille was exhausted and was incapable of getting across the traverse on his own. He asked if I thought it would be a good idea to swing him across on the snow to spare him the effort and give him a chance to get over the crisis. I agreed, adding that they should get a move on, because otherwise not only would we fail to reach the Gamba hut, we should not even reach the foot of the Rochers Grüber.

I turned back to Kohlmann. From the babble above I guessed that they were swinging Vieille across on the rope, and settled down to wait for the next man to descend. Half an hour went by. Not only had no one abseiled down, but the voices above were gradually falling silent. I was disconcerted. Was every abseil going to take as long as this? I climbed back up the rope until I could see the others and shouted: "Why aren't you coming?" A voice, perhaps Gallieni's, echoed by Mazeaud's, replied: "Vieille's dying." I was thunderstruck. The little group was huddled around the body of the dying man, which looked like a dark bundle against the whiteness of the snow at this end of the traverse. I went back down to Kohlmann without telling him what was happening. More time passed, perhaps twenty minutes. There were no more voices to be heard, only the sound of the wind. It had started snowing again. We stood in silent and terrible agony in the wan light. I climbed up again, to find that Vieille had died. My

companions were anchoring the body to a piton together with Gallieni's rucksack filled with equipment
that was no longer needed. There were no laments. It
was 10 o'clock. Kohlmann still did not understand what
had happened. I prepared him for the blow as best I
could, then Mazeaud arrived and conveyed the truth to
him in a series of half-statements. The shock was severe,
and he wept.

The descent began again. Taking advantage of a
moment when all six of us were attached to the same
piton, I recommended the maximum possible speed to
everybody, emphasizing the point by adding crudely:
"Otherwise we'll all go the same way as Vieille."
Oggioni brought up the rear and was a tower of strength
as always. Like Mazeaud, Guillaume and myself, he
carried a loaded rucksack, while Gallieni took turns at
relieving us all. Mazeaud continually encouraged and
urged on his compatriots.

About midday we heard voices. I had just abseiled
away from my companions, and at first thought that it
was they who were calling. Soon, however, I was convinced that rescuers were shouting up from below, in
this case a group of Courmayeur guides. It is laid down
in the constitution of this company of guides, to which I
belonged at that time, that all members are bound to go
to the help of a colleague in danger and have the right
to expect it in case of need. I yelled back and told the
others to shout in unison so as to be certain of being
heard. After this we felt better as we continued to
descend.

Nothing remarkable occurred until we were almost at

the foot of the Rochers Grüber. At this point, however, while I was trying to hammer in the umpteenth piton for the last rappel, Oggioni had the first of the attacks which were to prove fatal to him. A muffled cry at my shoulder made me spin around just in time to grab him as he came sliding unconscious down the last few metres of rope. I had already noticed during the last few rappels that he had followed very close behind me, almost alien to the operations of descent. Poor Andrea: now that I took a good look at him for the first time since the retreat had begun, I could see how much he had suffered. His features were tensed into a bitter semblance of a smile, his eyes defeated. It was obvious that he was using up the last remnants of his strength. I wanted to question him, to encourage him, but what could a man say or do who was in the same state as himself? We took a long, disconsolate look at one another. The final slither and leap over what passed for the bergschrund were accomplished with the aid of a long single rope that I held over my shoulders with all my strength while the others slid down it one by one. Thus we reached the Fresnay glacier at last at 3.30 p.m. I calculated that between starting the descent the previous morning and this moment we had done at least fifty abseils.

A gap in the cloud showed us the whole surface of the chaotic Fresnay glacier. It was unbelievable so much snow had fallen. But there was no sign of life, not even a track. Whence then did the voices come? I was to learn from the newspapers that the search party had looked for us on the Col de Fresnay. But why there, when everyone knew that we were on the central pillar? The

message we had left at the Bivouac de la Fourche indi-
cating our goal had been found by Gigi Panei and made
known as soon as the alarm was raised. We relapsed into
the blackest despair. Perhaps it was all up with us. We
had been convinced that the voices came from the base
of the Rochers Grüber—it was logical to think so—and
this idea had given us the strength to overcome all the
difficulties of that perilous descent. Now, however, we
were alone, with a long and terrible route still before us
to reach the Gamba hut.

We set off on the slow and painful descent of the
glacier, refusing to accept our bad luck. The snow was as
deep as ever; in my whole experience of winter mountaineering I could not remember having seen the like.
What we left behind us was not a trail but a trench.
Fortunately the cloud was rising and visibility slowly
improved. I yielded up the lead to Mazeaud, and we
entered the maze of crevasses through which we had to
find our way towards the Col de l'Innominata, the last
high barrier between us and salvation. I felt as though I
were dying of weariness, pain and cold, but refused to
let go. The line stretched out. Sometimes last, sometimes
next but last, every few steps Oggioni collapsed into the
snow, exhausted, though Gallieni was now carrying his
sack. Bound to one another with the rope, we groped our
way down the glacier in disorder, drunk with fatigue. It
became clear to me that in these circumstances there was
little likelihood of our reaching the Col de l'Innominata
in daylight. Immediately behind me, Gallieni seemed
the freshest of the party. I decided that we two should
go on as quickly as possible in order to reach the icy

gully below the Col de l'Innominata before it was too
late. It was absolutely essential to have done with the
rope and piton manœuvres before night should fall.

The others followed in our tracks led by Mazeaud,
followed by Kohlmann, Oggioni and Guillaume, in that
order. Meanwhile I got to grips with the extremely
difficult ice that coated the already difficult gully,
fighting with a kind of cold fury, since in half an hour it
would be dark. When the others reached us we roped up
again as a single party with myself in the lead seconded
by Gallieni, then Oggioni, Mazeaud and Kohlmann.
Guillaume had not appeared, and I learnt afterwards
that he had died in Oggioni's arms on the glacier. I
reached the Col de l'Innominata in total darkness. It was
past 9 o'clock on Saturday evening, and we had now
been out for six days. It was snowing again, and to
westward the flashes of yet another thunderstorm were
getting nearer. Snow and ice had filled and buried every
crack and flake of rock, and since I could find nowhere
to place a piton to belay my companions I had perforce
to hold the rope over my shoulder. I exhorted them to
make haste, but the operation proved both slow and
painful. The orders were punctuated with exclamations
of pain and despair. Behind Gallieni, Oggioni seemed
unable to climb any farther. Held on the rope from
above, Gallieni tried to help him in every possible way.
Down below, the two French were shouting and raving.
It was a scene of total chaos.

Three hours dragged by and we were still on the same
spot. I was unable to shift my position, since every so
often I received such a jerk on the rope that I was almost

catapulted over the edge, and on top of that I was almost fainting with the cold and the pain of the rope cutting into my flesh. If I gave way, it would be the end of the road for all of us. In the whole of these three hours Oggioni had not succeeded in moving an inch, and nothing that anybody could say to him seemed to have any effect. His only response was an occasional groan; it was as though he were in a trance. Somewhere en route he had clipped on to a piton with a karabiner, and now that he had to undo it before he could be hoisted upwards he had no strength left. Perhaps he had reached the point where he could no longer work out the connections. I wanted to climb down to him, but had no option but to hold firm to the rope which bound me to Gallieni. At last I decided on the extreme but only remaining course of leaving the others where they were, and descending rapidly with Gallieni to get help from the Gamba hut, where there would certainly be a rescue party. Now that I saw the necessity, I realized that I should have saved precious time by coming to this conclusion earlier. I therefore shouted down to the others that Oggioni should remain belayed by the powerful Mazeaud, and in a couple of hours at the most we would all be saved. While these manœuvres were going on Kohlmann suddenly broke loose and emerged out of the darkness, hauling himself arm over arm up the rope that hung down the ice-polished gully, clambering over Mazeaud, Oggioni and Gallieni in a kind of fury. Sensing his frenzy, the latter succeeded in clipping him to the rope with a karabiner as he went by, presumably unaware that I was only holding the rope over my shoulder.

Presently the three of us stood together on the Col de l'Innominata. Kohlmann exclaimed that he was hungry and thirsty, then asked: "Where's the hut?" He was obviously out of his mind, but we could not leave him alone on the col. We therefore tied him on between us, and Gallieni began the descent. When Kohlmann's turn came, he seemed to have forgotten every measure of caution. The gully was steep and coated in ice. We had not gone far when we came across a thin 60 metre rope which, hidden by a spike of rock, hung down from a piton on the col behind us. Later we learned that it had generously been left on the other side of the col the first day by the American John Harlin and the German Kirsch with the aim of helping either a party of Swiss caught by the bad weather on the Punta Gugliermina, or should we still be alive, ourselves, in the event of any of us retreating that way. But why was it now hanging on this side of the col instead of in the right place on the other side, where it would have solved our problems and saved lives? For better or worse we slid down it, then continued as best we could. Kohlmann was becoming more and more of a liability. He simply lay down and let himself slide as I lowered him from an unsecured shoulder belay, and remained hanging on the rope as I climbed down in my turn. I would then stop. Eventually the rope would go slack, showing that he had found a place to hold on, but as I started down again an unexpected tug would show that he had slipped off once more, so that there was a constant risk of our all being dragged down together. Neither encouragement nor insult seemed to have any effect. He uttered meaningless phrases and waved his arms. We had expected to reach the hut in an hour, but with Kohlmann in this condition three had gone by already.

At last we reached the bottom of the gully and carried on to the end of the little Châtelet glacier. To reach the hut we had only to cross a few hummocks of no danger or difficulty apart from the toil of ploughing through the deeply drifted snow. Our only thought was to get to the Gamba hut; our spirits began to revive. Suddenly, however, a new problem intervened. One of Gallieni's gloves came off, and as he bent to look for it he slid his hand inside his anorak to keep it warm. Kohlmann must have thought that he was about to draw a pistol, and tackled him with outstretched arms. Entwined together they rolled down the slope. I tightened the rope to impede Kohlmann's movements so that Gallieni could wriggle free. Kohlmann then flung himself at me. I dodged, and he fell at my feet twisting and raving. He had gone mad. Scrambling up, he tried to fling himself on us, but as long as both of us held the rope in tension there was nothing he could do. The three of us were bound together inextricably. We could not drag him towards the hut, yet it was imperative not to lose an unnecessary minute. Somehow we had to get clear of our poor crazy friend who crouched, watching every movement we made, waiting to leap on us at the first opportunity. The knots with which we had tied on were frozen iron hard; there was no hope of undoing them. Neither of us had a knife with which to cut free. Each in turn therefore held the rope in his teeth and lowered his breeches so as to slip his waistloop down over his thighs. Somehow we managed to do this without Kohlmann understanding what we were up to. All of a sudden I yelled to Gallieni: "Slack! Go!" Rolling and tumbling in the snow, we ran as hard as we could towards the hut, which we were sure of reaching in a few minutes. The place where we had left Kohlmann was absolutely safe; he could not possibly fall off. Alas, those who went to his rescue were just in time to witness his last breath.

Like two bits of human wreckage, almost on all fours amid the dark, clinging snow, we butted up against the hut at last. There was not a light to be seen. The dark, indistinct shape was like that of any one of a thousand blocks of granite on the moraine, and I had found it only because I knew the surroundings like the interior of my own house. We staggered around the framework building beating on the shutters with our bare hands. As we reached the doorway, steps were heard inside and someone lifted the latch. The door hinged open and we saw the interior full of sleeping forms dimly lit by a guttering candle. I peered at a few faces without recognizing any. Suddenly someone sprang up and cried: "Walter! Is it you?" There was a general tumult. The missing men had finally succeeded in finding those who had gone out to look for them. Gallieni was there safe and sound at my side.

I shouted above the hubbub: "Hurry! There's another one just outside! The others are on the far side of the Col de l'Innominata! Get a move on!" It was 3 o'clock on Sunday morning. The blizzard was blowing as fiercely as ever. I stretched out on the table. They unbuckled our frozen crampons, undressed us, clothed us in dry garments, gave us hot drinks. I fell into a profound sleep.

When I next awoke, three hours had gone by and it was light. The door was creaking open, and behind the threshold the profiles of two men were outlined against the greyness. One of them approached and embraced me; it was my friend Gaston Rébuffat, who had just arrived from Chamonix by helicopter. Then he spoke words that I shall never forget while I live: "Oggioni's dead. They're bringing him down now." I was overcome by uncontrollable grief. The bodies of my poor companions were recovered one by one, except for that of Vieille, which remained inaccessible for another week. Mazeaud, the only survivor, threw his arms around me and we cried together.

Lying in bed, I leafed through the newspapers. The sensationally headlined dispatches and features concerning "the missing party on the central pillar of Mont Blanc" had multiplied day by day. Then came the terrible news: four dead, Bonatti saved. From this contrast arose an absurd situation. In the accounts written for public consumption, facts, personalities and words were misrepresented, distorted and muddled until they sometimes ended up representing the exact opposite of the truth. The anguish of the survivors was taken for delirium, their reticence or spontaneous homage to their dead friends for an expression of cowardice or even guilt. There was talk of legal proceedings, questions in parliament, proposals devoid of scruple or common sense.

What was happening was paradoxical and grotesque. In the midst of my pain, exhaustion and sense of loss, despite my clear conscience as a man and as a mountain guide, I found myself having to struggle to preserve my character from the stupid accusations thrown up against it by public opinion. It was as though the public, always more swift to blame than praise, could not express its compassion for the dead other than to the detriment of the living.

Very often it is the man in the street whose emptiness or morbid obsessions encourage speculation and sensational reporting, but it must also be said that in the quest for "news" the information media are generally pitiless. So it came about that by a sort of artificially worked-up chain reaction everybody began to judge and criticize the whole tragic affair, to allocate responsibility, and to lay down what I should have done. Just like five years earlier, when I had been involved in a winter ascent of Mont Blanc which had also had tragic consequences,* there were interviews and round-table discussions in the press, on the radio and on television where Professor X, the well-known actor Y, the professional man Z and the honourable K gave their views or even sat in judgement on myself, my companions, and our actions and mistakes. All this while the survivors still lay in agony in their hospital beds.

Why all this furore? In the first place, undoubtedly,

---

* *Translator's note:* Not in Bonatti's own party. He refers to the death of the Belgian students Vincendon and Henry, who happened by coincidence to be on the mountain at the same time, and whom he did his best to save.

it was due to the power and suggestiveness of the press, associated above all with the irresponsibility of those who sometimes write insinuating, partial or poisonous "pieces" or "sketches". If I have any good name left, it is certainly not to them that I owe it. Misinformed readers who are thus provoked into writing letters reflecting these deceptions—a human reaction—are equally victims. The proof is in the verbal echoes such as "unnatural and fool-hardy actions", "brought upon their own heads", "unable to waste any sympathy", "deserve sentence of hard labour", and so on. A depressing brand of moral indifference wrapped up in moralizing came to the fore, the fruit of an ignoble system of information. It would be a serious matter if every subject of concern to the press were treated in the same way. In the interests of truth I must add that there were journalists who wrote accurately, objectively and sensitively. But not many.

Whether it pleases others or not, the simple fact is that the seven of us were up there on the pillar in the pursuit of an ideal, and despite pain and exhaustion fought bravely at one another's side against the unrelenting bad luck that cut us off from the world in a death-trap where no one was able to bring us help until right at the end. If I had survived, it was perhaps because I had a stronger will to live than the others, or owed it to them not to give way. Subsequently, Mazeaud was to write that he owed me his life and that but for me all six would have died, and the French Government awarded me its highest official recognition, membership of the Légion d'Honneur, "for courage and fraternal

solidarity in dramatic circumstances". But as I lay there
in my hospital bed still under the shadow of the wing of
death, this "civilized" society in which I also have my
place turned and unjustly tore out my heart. I wondered
if my body would accept a higher rate of renitrogena-
tion but for the relentless emotional attrition that was
fed with new matter day by day; it seemed that those
few days had shortened my life by ten years. Such an
experience either destroys or affects a man profoundly,
so that he returns to life changed, understanding more
than before. "Civilized man" is able to inflict moral
violence no less painful than physical torture. This I have
learnt and paid for to the full in my own person.

The force of the will to survive is astounding. Day by
day I recovered my physical and mental powers, and
presently my gaze began to turn again longingly to the
jagged outlines of Mont Blanc. The day we left hospital
Mazeaud and I promised each other to return to the
central pillar and finish off those remaining 80 metres.
For us the project was like a religious pilgrimage to
complete a monument to the courage and sacrifice of our
dead friends.

It was hoping for too much; we were to receive a rude
awakening from our dream. Even if all men were sensitive to certain values, their feelings would still be under-
mined by the ruthless law of ambition and success. Thus,
as soon as the weather had settled, barely a couple of
weeks after the tragedy, the pillar was attempted by a
Franco-Italian party. Not us, naturally; we were not yet

fit enough. The two climbers landed on the summit of Mont Blanc by helicopter, then descended the Peuterey ridge and attacked the pillar. Three days later they turned back. The pillar remained unclimbed for the time being, but the last shadow of reserve had vanished. Owing to the publicity surrounding the tragedy this monolith had suddenly become the goal of some of the toughest mountaineers in the world. The spell of bad weather gave place to an unusually hot, dry summer, and Mont Blanc had never looked so clear of snow. Was it pure chance, or was fate mocking us?

On 29 August 1961, eight men of four different nationalities finally succeeded in violating the top of the pillar after a stiff fight. Not content with thus defiling the graves of my four poor friends, certain of the party claimed to have rendered "homage to the victims". But up there, Oggioni, Guillaume, Kohlmann and Vieille had above all been comrades and partners, and no helicopter had taken off on their behalf until it was time to transport their bodies back to the valley. They died purely for a pure ideal, and held to an ethic throughout. It would have been preferable not to profane such an example.

Through a long convalescence I slowly recovered enough strength to return to the mountains, taking long walks through the woods, then doing harder and higher climbs. At last came the final test, Mont Blanc by the diagonal route and Mont Maudit by the Kagami route. These two ice-climbs on the broad Brenva flank had not been repeated since they were first ascended in 1932*

---

* *Translator's note: sic.* Actually 1937. See Brown, G.: *Brenva* (Dent) for details.

- - - - - - The line of the ill-fated attempt on the central pillar of
Fresnay.
——————— The Bonatti–Zappelli direct route on the south face of
Mont Blanc (22 September 1961).

Noon on 11 July 1961. The beginning of the fatal storm.

The Bonatti–Mazeaud route on the east face of the Petites Jorasses (10–11 July 1963).

and 1929 respectively. This not only fulfilled my long-standing plan to do all the Brenva routes, of which there were fifteen at that time, but also proved to my own satisfaction that I was finally back on form and fit to try anything.

On 29 August 1961 the central pillar of Fresnay was climbed. I filed it away in my memory and turned my attention to the still-virgin face between the right-hand pillar and the Peuterey ridge. The face rose directly to the summit of Mont Blanc de Courmayeur. It promised neither airy bivouacs nor the ultimate in gymnastic rock-climbing, but simply a superb, logical line up a harmonious succession of rock and ice. It resembled one of those nineteenth-century ascents which were climbed in order to reach a summit in the days when equipment consisted of a rope, an axe, strong legs, plenty of courage and wrists which would stand up to cutting thousands of steps. To find an unclimbed face out of another age rising 800 metres to the highest summit in Europe was both incredible and exciting. I had been looking at it for years, and I would have gone for it two months earlier had I guessed that I was to be involved in any Franco-Italian rivalry for the central pillar.

The 20 September was a hot, clear, end-of-summer day which gave place to a night of bitter cold. This striking change between the shortening days and lengthening nights is normal at that season, and if the barometer indicates settled fine weather there is no better time for undertaking rapid climbs. I had therefore walked up to the now deserted Gamba hut and lay in the sunlight revolving memories until the nocturnal frost

D

should have locked the stones into their mountain bed.

My companion was Cosimo Zappelli. Twenty-eight years old, he was descended from a family of sailors in Viareggio, but climbing was his vocation. I understood. Like me, he had left his home town to live at the foot of Mont Blanc. After the tragedy on the pillar I had offered him the other end of my rope, and from that time on he was my second in almost all my climbs until, three years later, he entered the Courmayeur company of guides from which I had resigned. Between it and me there was neither understanding nor communication. I knew that his choice was human and ineluctable, yet somehow I was disappointed. Perhaps he had not succeeded in gathering the fruit of my experience; perhaps, more simply, we were just two different people. I therefore stopped climbing with him, retaining nothing from our partnership but excellent memories.

At 3.30 a.m. the darkness was total, the air freezing. We found our way up to the Col de l'Innominata by the faint light of our head-torches. As it was still dark it seemed best to wait a little, so we settled down in silence just on the far side of the col and wriggled into our sleeping-bags. A slight breeze whispered among the rocks; the stars shone and twinkled. Now and again the heavy rumble of a sérac rose from the Fresnay glacier. Everything was quite normal, but inwardly I was re-living the tragedy, struggling to overcome the tremendous psychological incubus which seemed to fetter me to the spot. At last light came into the sky. As I slid down the first rappel I found first one and then another piton that I had placed that tragic evening, groping over the ice-glazed rock in the thickening gloom. That it should now all be so easy! Below me the glacier was terribly devoid of snow, covered in tottering séracs. One of them was particularly impressive. At this range it looked like a white pillar lying poised in balance on its side across the glacier, yet we should have to run right underneath it.

I told Zappelli of a strange incident that had occurred to me a year earlier on the Fresnay glacier, the most dangerous in this locality. I had been with Dr Gysi, a Swiss client, at the place which the Courmayeur guides call the "Brogliatta",* which lies just below where we now sat. For lack of any alternative, we were crossing a wide sérac. In order to get him to hurry up, I told him how precisely at this spot the famous guide Lionel Terray and his client had been crossing below an apparently stable sérac when it gave way. As everyone knows, séracs and crevasses always recur in the same places because the tortuous course of the underlying bed affects the relatively fluid ice of the glacier in the same way as the obstacles on the bed of a river create rapids. On that occasion Terray had had a miraculous escape, but his companion† was killed. No sooner had I finished telling Gysi about this than we were both thrown into the air, landing heavily on our backs. As though in an earthquake, the enormous sérac had settled several metres vertically, but without tipping over, a veritable miracle.

Perhaps on account of this spine-chilling story, Zappelli and I hurried anxiously under our sérac, which

* *Translator's note:* Roughly equivalent to "mess" in this context.
† The British mountaineer Gerard Cruikshank.

resembled a Parthenon poised to topple. It must have been a good 100 metres long. At this point occurred an incident which subsequently gave me a good deal of food for thought. Hardly had we got past the danger point when a terrifying crash made us spin around. There followed a moment of utter stillness in the mountain cirque and in ourselves; then, accompanied by a terrific blast, the whole ice-temple trembled from base to top, swelled, and finally exploded into a boiling, thundering cloud that rolled down over us. When all was silent again and everything lay still as though nothing had happened, Zappelli and I looked at each other unable to speak a word.

From the ice-fall of the Fresnay glacier we reached the warmth of the sun on the ridge beside the Punta Gugliermina in a little over an hour. The long crest rising from there to the Aiguille Blanche de Peuterey and on to the summit of Mont Blanc bewitched me as always. Slender, dominating, slung from peak to peak, it winds upwards like a fringe loosely fixed here and there, and the white slopes on the Brenva side extend solemnly like an ermine cloak. A few clouds flamed in the sky that stretched out silent and blue to the remotest horizon. In the valleys far below were gathered cocoons of autumn mist, soon to be evaporated by the sun.

By midday we were on the Aiguille Blanche, and an hour later on the Col de Peuterey. This was as far as we were going for the day, so we stretched out and basked in the feeble warmth of the sunlight at 4,000 metres.

The first of the many times I had been here was in 1953, also in September. I was making my first ascent of

Bonatti on the north face of the Grand Pilier d'Angle.

On the vertical, ice-encrusted rock band of the north face of the
Grand Pilier d'Angle.

Mont Blanc, and it was not by accident that I had come this way: the central pillar had already begun to fascinate me, as did the south face which we were now going to attack. On that day too, I remembered, Roberto Bignami and I had reached the col early via the couloir on its Brenva side, and like today the sky had been bright and solemn. We were alone on the great mountain. We had spent the afternoon sunbathing, chatting of a thousand things, daydreaming, listening to the infinite silence of the heights. Now everything looked just the same, as though time had stopped. Yet so many things had changed: experiences that I would not wish to repeat, faces I should not see again. Bignami himself had vanished among the peaks of the Himalaya.

Shortly after 4 o'clock the sun dropped behind the Brouillard ridge, and an hour later the snow was already frozen. We wandered along the flank of the mountain to look for a way across the bergschrund. The face towered above us. To the left, silhouetted against the cold, faded sky, rose the challenging spire of the central pillar. Suddenly, unexpectedly, a feeling of dismay came over me. I looked around. There was the crevasse where we had spent our last bivouac, the slope where Vieille had died, the Rochers Grüber, the shadowy Fresnay glacier, and far below in the violet evening light the little gully of the Innominata. But I was not seeing only the mountain. There were men staggering bowed and silent through the bottomless snow, falling and helping each other up again like dying drunkards. Wherever I looked I saw the same vision. I felt an invading sadness and a desire to flee from this obsessive, haunted world.

A quarter past two in the morning. The huge three-quarter moon was sinking behind the black profile of Mont Blanc. The stars shone brilliantly. We were getting ready to leave the col. The cold was paralyzing, the silence so intense as to numb the mind. Presently the need for action distracted me from the demented thoughts that had thronged my head all night. The slope was steep, frozen crystal-hard and crackling underfoot. At times we had to cut steps. Dawn reached us already at the foot of the rocks high up on the face. The red disk of the sun rose prodigiously above the horizon, smoking as though exhaling residual gases after the creation; a new-made, generous sun that we worshipped like savages.

In the conditions in which we found it, the climbing was safe and full of pleasure. We tried to keep to the most direct line possible. Three pitons sank ringing into the red granite of a high corner in the middle of the difficulties, then the way went straight up broken rock to the summit of the Mont Blanc de Courmayeur.

Walking back down the Val Veni that evening, I looked up at the proud flank shining in the moonlight. It seemed impossible that we should have just descended from those heights.

II

The Grand Pilier d'Angle

As I came back down to the valley after climbing the north face of the Grandes Jorasses in August 1949, my mind was still impressed with the vertiginous, beetling ice-slopes, and my bones still felt shivery from successive bivouacs at 4,000 metres. I was thus in a state to appreciate nothing but flat, warm, safe places, and all forms of comfort and repose. In this condition I was walking across the meadows of Entrèves, which in those days was still a pretty Alpine village, when somebody pointed out the Grand Pilier d'Angle towering above the Brenva glacier, and said that a party had just succeeded in climbing those icy boilerplates. The idea was enough to induce cold shudders, as at that time I could witness better than anybody. Across the eight kilometres of air that separated me from them, I almost seemed to be able to pick out their profiles. But who were these unknown individuals who had dared so much? Beside what they had achieved I felt small indeed. As time went on I learnt that the leader had been the formidable Austrian climber Hermann Buhl, and the incident began to seem more credible. The great admiration I have always felt for him dates from that time.

As the years went by and I became more familiar with Mont Blanc, I realized the misunderstanding.

What Buhl and his companion Martin Schliessler had climbed on that occasion was the slippery north face of the Aiguille Blanche de Peuterey, a superb ice route; but in comparison the Grand Pilier d'Angle, which I had now scrutinized from practically every angle, was of a different order.

Nevertheless it staggered me that this colossal pillar, the highest rock face overlooking the Brenva basin, was still unclimbed from this side. Curiously resembling the prow of a ship, it juts a kilometre high over the glacier to an altitude of 4,200 metres.

The Pilier d'Angle or Eckpfeiler has an east face looking down towards Entrèves, an impressive north-east spur, and a hidden north face of which only the profile can be seen from the valley. Whereas this last is shadowed and seamed with ice like a monstrous spider's web, the north-east corner is clean-cut and composed of beautiful russet granite. However, it is the east face which has given the pillar its reputation. Pale and mutilated, it is the tottering remains of one of the biggest landslips to have occurred in the Alps in historical times. On 14 November 1920 a huge avalanche occurred on the east flank of the pillar, crashing into the hanging glacier which in those days reached to just below the Col de Peuterey, and rocking it to its foundations. But this was only the prelude to the real catastrophe. Five days later, as in an apocalyptic vision, the whole upper edge of the pillar, a flank at least 500 metres high, came thundering down into the upper bay of the Brenva glacier, continuing on down with renewed impetus and devastating force into the forest at the foot of the Val Veni. Since that time the face seems to have been slowly stabilizing, but the rock-falls are still considerable. The pillar was first climbed on 1–3 August 1957 via its compact north-east spur by Toni Gobbi and myself, an elegant and difficult route in grandiose surroundings which is described in my first book.* Thus the Grand Pilier d'Angle became part of the long story of the conquest of Mont Blanc. No sooner had I done this ascent, however, than it produced a strangely exciting effect in me, as though, after cutting a delicious fruit in two, I had been unable to taste it. Obviously, it was true that the north-east spur divided the north and east faces from one another, thus creating two problems of an entirely different nature, one entirely of rock and open to the sun, the other entirely of ice and shut off from it.

As the years went by and my knowledge of high mountains grew, I became convinced that the north face of the Grand Pilier d'Angle represented the greatest concentration of extreme difficulties that could be found. Without any doubt it was the gloomiest, wildest, most dangerous face of mixed rock and ice that I had ever seen in the Alps. Bands of smooth and often overhanging rock, completely encrusted with ice or unstable snow, alternated with ice-slopes of dizzying steepness, the entire flank being menaced at all times by overhanging séracs and cornices that burst over it. A 1,000 metre funnel of cold light, this concave inferno creates in the mountaineer a feeling of continual apprehension. But the weather is perhaps the key factor. A climber caught

* *Le mie montagne*, Zanichelli, Bologna 1961: published in English as *On the Heights* (Hart-Davies, 1964).

by storm or thaw above the first third of the wall would be unable to turn back. Either he would have to try to reach the top as quickly as possible, a highly problematical solution, or else he would have to remain where he was, in the sway of the elements at around 4,000 metres, virtually condemned to freeze to death or be swept off by an avalanche. Without any doubt it is the most impregnable bastion of Mont Blanc. I knew all this very well; yet, impelled by that mysterious impulse which has always urged mankind towards the unknown, I felt an irresistible desire to measure myself against it.

There are only two conditions in which this face can be attempted with much hope of success. The first is when abundant snow covers the ice-slopes, so that they can be climbed relatively rapidly. But this means that the rock bands and even the overhangs will be plastered with an insecure and dangerous layer of ice. The second solution, therefore, is to attack when the rock is as clear as possible; but precisely for this reason, it entails an even greater peril than the first, inasmuch as following the thaw the ice-slopes will have shed their snow also and will remain hard as crystal, calling for much step-cutting and consequent loss of energy and above all of time, so that the climber will remain mortally exposed to the frequent cannonade of ice and rock for a much longer period. By the very nature of the flank, perfect hybrid conditions with good rock and good snow together will never be found, since each excludes the other.

Even for the most expert, therefore, an undertaking of this order calls for a combination of boldness, caution and great peace of mind, three qualities which are the fruit of a thorough and conscientious preparation. This state of grace must necessarily coincide with perfect conditions on the mountain. This was the case towards the middle of September 1961, and Zappelli and I therefore decided to attack.

A half-moon was rising as we reached Col Moore at 2 o'clock in the morning. It was a night of frozen splendour, exactly what we needed for our venture. The col is a veritable observation post over the Brenva cirque, like an African treetop platform for observing wild animals. Only here the wild beasts are the roaring séracs which assert their dominion as they go thundering down the giant precipices. On our right, the majestic Brenva face now lay silent and still as though the beasts were sleeping, and the glacier below disappeared amid the hard shadows lower down the mountain. But if the moonlight seemed to render the surroundings almost harmless, it gave the Grand Pilier d'Angle opposite us a truly fearful appearance. By some trick of perspective the north face seemed absolutely vertical, and the hanging glacier appeared to stick out so far as to be ready to tumble on our heads at any moment, white, shining, utterly smooth, like an absurd slate 1,000 metres high. It made me shudder. Though I knew full well that this was an illusion, and that the mountain was in perfect condition, this diabolical vision somehow rooted me to the spot. Hypnotized, I stood in silence for half an hour, while Zappelli, like a good pupil, said nothing. Suddenly I was surprised to hear myself saying: "No, I don't want to leave my hide up there."

So we turned back. At home, I could find no rational

explanation for my decision. I had had all the trumps in my hand, and the face had never shown its weaknesses so clearly. Yet I had turned tail. What an amazing mechanism the human psyche is! It can invent anything, even miracles. Now in some mysterious way, perhaps by a capricious combination of circumstances, it had succeeded in rousing in me emotional reactions destructive of all logic, an irrational and irresistible panic of which I myself had been the victim. Well, that too was an experience.

Winter passed, and very early, in mid-June, the mountain lowered its guard. The snow was plentiful and compact, it froze hard at night, and there was a full moon. By a stroke of luck our preparations were already complete. On the night of 19 June we reached the base of the pillar, but at this point the barometric pressure unexpectedly dropped. Was bad weather on the way? Despite the starry sky, this doubt was enough to make us turn back. Nor had I any reason to regret the decision: a few hours later, at dawn, it began to snow. Luckily the storm was short-lived, and two days later we again stood at the foot of the face. This time all the auguries were good. The three-quarter moon had just risen, and its rays slanting across the flank of the pillar exaggerated the appearance of difficulty, frightening me again, which was natural enough in the circumstances. But this time I knew enough to control myself.

The first problem was the bergschrund, which was continuous and very wide. Its upper edge was formed by an overhanging wall of ice 20 metres high. In vain I sought for a weak point in its defences. Finally I had to

Bonatti finishing out the long traverse on the east face of the Grand
Pilier d'Angle.

The three Bonatti routes on the Grand Pilier d'Angle:
. . . . . . the north-east spur (1–3 August 1957)
——— the north face (22 June 1962)
- - - - - - the east face (11–12 October 1963).

resolve on an extreme manœuvre which had proved effective in other cases. Lowering myself into the crevasse, I cut a spiral tunnel through to the slopes above. It was a horrible job. For two hours I hacked away, covered in ice-chips and frozen débris, until at last I emerged.

It was 1 o'clock in the morning of 22 June. Before me rose vertiginous slopes of frozen snow, furrowed with deep avalanche trenches, clear witness to what happened here in the warmer hours. I began to cut steps diagonally up to the right, belaying at the end of each runout so that Zappelli could follow. Gradually we penetrated farther into the zone where the crossfire from the séracs bordering the Pear buttress and those impending above us on our own face converged. The nervous tension reached a pitch such that there was no need to look up in order to realize what might happen at any moment; the ice-fall would be felt in the heart and the blood even before it was heard. Every puff of wind or creak of the slope made us jump. The avalanches that I had seen descending these slopes were of monstrous proportions, at least 400 metres wide, raising a white cloud half a kilometre high and setting off a blast that in itself would have been sufficient to kill a man.

We had now rounded the last of the spurs of rock which form a pedestal to the face, and henceforward were completely exposed to the avalanches. The moonlight illuminated the notorious séracs of the Pear and the Route Major with sinister clarity. "Hurry, hurry," I kept repeating to myself. But whatever I might say, I was obliged to chip a little notch for a foothold at every step. In some places the snow was so worn down by the avalanches that it was no more than a treacherous, marble-hard coating that mimicked the ice on which it lay, and in such spots each pace seemed to take an eternity. Meanwhile the slope was getting steeper and steeper, and the moon was sinking behind the mountain, so that we entered a zone of deep shadow. Switching on our head-torches, we continued. I sensed the face glooming above my head, but could pick out no detail. It was just a great, shapeless, measureless mass. Nevertheless I had to guess our way towards the feature which, in the course of studying the face, we had called "the twisting rib". This was an essential feature of the route, and it was vital that I should hit if off. Yet another cause of anxiety was the fact that every metre we climbed took us farther from the possibility of retreat.

Came the dawn. Here was the twisting rib; my route-finding had been spot-on. But now that I could clearly see our surroundings, they terrified me. We were right in the heart of the Grand Pilier d'Angle. The slope fell away vertiginously between our feet down, down, down to the still-dark glacier. A hundred metres above us, beyond the twisting rib, the way was barred by a band of vertical rock, overhanging in places but still plastered with ice, resembling a face in the Patagonian Andes. However, there was no alternative: we should just have to climb it direct. To retreat at this point would perhaps be more dangerous than to go on.

I was just about to start up the twisting rib when there was a heavy report. An avalanche from the upper séracs of the Route Major was descending in one bound of nearly 1,000 metres, bursting and setting up a swirling blast as though it wanted to bring the sky down on top of it. Although I was now out of range, I felt my muscles tense with fear as I saw the avalanche sweep down the Brenva face and spill out on to the glacier, covering the route we had followed during the night. The ensuing cloud of ice-particles came boiling up and enveloped us.

The twisting rib proved to be of no particular difficulty, and an hour later we found ourselves under the redoubted slanting band which bars the entire face and is the crux of the ascent. Even at its thinnest point, it is at least 120 metres high. The rocks were completely white in their armour of ice and snow. I therefore set about trying to clear them with the axe so as to find holds and cracks where I could plant pitons. It was terribly laborious. The few pitons I was able to place penetrated the clear ice with which the cracks were obstructed only with difficulty. Not once did we have any real security. The holds, when you could find them, were glassy and polished. The points of my crampons biting into ice-glaze were our best guarantee of safety, and I therefore kept them on throughout. From me to the glacier it would have been one clear bound of perhaps 500 metres.

After the sun had been up for an hour or so it began to warm the atmosphere, and as the frost became less tenacious stones and lumps of ice started to whistle past. I was struck several times, but luckily my helmet protected my head. In these conditions I continued climbing, but those terrible 120 metres took five hours to overcome. Right at the start of this key passage I had been obliged to take off my gloves in order to get a better grip, and the continual impact against the sharp-grained ice soon cut my fingers so that you could almost have followed our route from the bloodstains. Nevertheless I continued to win my way centimetre by centimetre. Tension reduced our dialogue to the strict minimum, fragments such as: "Watch that peg, it's not sound"; "Mind out, verglas"; "Can you see anything yet?"; "No, it's all the same, it just goes on being vertical"; "Warn me if you see anything big coming down". And so it went on for five hours without any let-up at all.

By 11 a.m. the great unknown of the slanting band lay below us. The face now leaned back, but precisely for this reason I was deprived of all cover and directly in the line of fire from the super-dangerous hanging séracs, through which a few rays of sunlight were filtering. It only needed the smallest fragment to detach itself and we should be swept off. At the tiniest sound my head would jerk upwards as I clung to the slope, instinctively seeking a rock under which to shelter even though I knew it would be no use. I was perfectly aware of the struggle I was having to control the panic that kept rising up in me. It was vitally urgent to find a way out of this obsessing danger. On our right was the strangulated, almost vertical groove down which the hanging glacier discharged. My decision was taken. Belaying to the last rock, I brought up Zappelli and without further ceremony began to hack a slightly rising traverse across the green ice of the drain.

The distance was 40 metres precisely, the same as the length of our rope. From the other side of the traverse a long and inviting rib of rock led upwards in perfect

The author and his style.

The Trident, the Chandelle, the Petit Clocher and the Grand Capucin seen against the backdrop of the Brenva face.

safety. Across the slippery intervening funnel I now made the most terrifying traverse of my life, nicking tiny notches just sufficient for me to remain in balance on the four front points of my crampons while I chipped the next. Anchored to the rock with a piton, Zappelli watched my every movement. The affair was rendered still more awkward by the heavy sack that hung from my shoulders. Should I lose my balance for an instant or should I be struck by a projectile from above, I would end up hanging in space, held from the piton by my companion. Luckily it did not happen. A few small lumps of ice smacked into me, but nothing of any consequence. It was certainly not the most orthodox way to tackle such a traverse, but it was the fastest, and that was what mattered here.

As I reached the other side of the groove, panting from the effort, something shot past my face, making me jump. It was a yellowy-brown butterfly, carried up here on some current of warm air and fated to die at the first breath of frost. Just at that moment, however, I envied him; while I had to make my way slowly, he had wings and could escape at once from that place of death.

There was not a moment to be lost. I yelled to Zappelli to leave behind the two pitons and to come across as quickly as he could. On the lower edge of the rock rib we were still in danger. The air was stiflingly warm, and we feverishly scrambled up 40 metres higher to a dry, safe ledge.

Here we at last permitted ourselves a short rest. I smiled as we hauled a flask of wine out of the sack, re-

E

membering for the first time that it was my birthday. Well, being up here was as good a way of celebrating as any other. We ate dates, prunes and a couple of vitamin C pills, and that seemed as fine a feast as a man could desire.

I calculated that we must be about half-way up the face. There could be no question of turning back, but on the other hand the major uncertainties were now behind us. Forty metres below, the face curved over, so that there was not even a background before the region of the Col du Géant, far-off and indistinct. Rarely had I been in such impressive surroundings. On the horizon lay a thin parchment of high cloud roughened by the wind. To both sides were smooth ice-slopes broken only by the outline of hanging séracs. We had bivouac equipment with us, but the very idea of passing the night on a face like this was enough to make us think of moving on. Fear had not made my hand or knee tremble in action, but now my nerves were worn and there was a tight feeling in my chest. I felt an urgent desire to escape from this inferno as quickly as possible.

We started climbing again over a series of ruddy-coloured buttresses with occasional overhangs. Higher up the going looked more difficult, and presently the shadow arrived, hardening forms and outlines. Soon my hands were freezing and the cold began to penetrate my body. The problem of finding a way off the face was becoming more complicated. The alternatives were either to force the snowed-up rocks directly above or else to traverse diagonally back across the ice-funnel to the upper part of the hanging glacier, and in the end I

opted for the latter solution. At this height the funnel
was about 80 metres across and consisted entirely of
black ice, so that we should have perhaps two pitches
of hard work with the axe. I started cutting. After 40
metres I tried to place a piton in a rock which projected
from the slope, but there were no cracks, so I was forced
to use an ice-piton instead. This did not offer much
security, as the sudden drop in temperature had rendered
the surface extremely brittle. I anchored myself as well
as possible, brought my companion across and set out
again across the middle of the funnel.

Following the heat of midday, the sudden frost was
causing the slabs of ice stuck to the overhangs to split
off. They came whizzing through the air, bursting into
fragments on the slope above us. This was all right so
long as we were only hit by the small shot, but presently
larger lumps began to come down. No sooner had I
succeeded in planting another ice-peg than a sound of
bursting blocks followed by a cry from Zappelli made
me spin around. A plate of ice had landed on his head.
Luckily he had had the reflex to hold on to the ice-piton,
and his crash-helmet had absorbed the blow. Had he
been knocked out and fallen, it would have been a bad
lookout for us both.

The danger was increasing every minute. I therefore
decided to hammer in a piton every few metres so as to
increase the degree of security in case another blow
should knock one or both of us off. Once again our nerves
were tense with apprehension, and indeed no more
than five minutes after Zappelli's shock the whole mountain began to tremble. A colossal avalanche of ice had

detached itself close up under the summit of Mont Blanc and came thundering down towards the hanging glacier of the Pear. This acted like a springboard, and the spectacle which then met my eyes remains engraved in memory as one of the most appalling I have ever seen. God knows that I am not exaggerating when I say that the avalanche reached almost to where we were clinging. Fortunately I remained motionless, in balance on the front points of my crampons, while my horrified gaze followed the cataclysm down out of sight. For several seconds the echoes rolled and rumbled, then a white cloud was borne up on the whirlwind, enveloping us in violet reflections. I felt tiny and fragile; but when calm returned and I looked down again I shuddered. The whole of the twisting rib up which we had climbed that morning was completely white with the débris of the avalanche.

The 40 metres of rope had now run out, but I had not reached the end of the traverse. I therefore brought my partner across on a tight rope and continued. Finally I emerged on to the hanging glacier above the ice-cliff. Here the snow was floury, deep, and ready to slide away in an avalanche, but before I could find a place to cross the schrund below the final section of the face I had to traverse almost the whole slope. Between us and the crest of the ridge there remained just 150 metres, but they consisted of extremely steep ice treacherously coated with powder snow. Truly, this face is an unrelenting series of problems piled one on another. I gathered my forces for this last effort. The short stretch of horizon visible in the east was wavering in the heat of the sun, yet up here the cold bit ever more deeply, so that our boots and clothes, saturated during the heat of the day, stiffened to a hard shell, rendering our movements short and almost clumsy. Crossing a last crevasse, I headed straight for the summit of the Grand Pilier d'Angle. At 6.5 p.m. I got my hands over it and hauled myself on to the crest. A new world opened up before my eyes. Directly in front was the profile of the central pillar of Fresnay and lower down the Col de Peuterey, the Aiguille Blanche, the crest of the Innominata, deep glaciers and, far below, green hills bathed in sunlight. Our colour-starved eyes feasted on the scene. There were a few more hours of daylight left, but we thought it best to settle down here on a comfortable ledge and wait until the nocturnal chill had hardened the fragile snowy crest of the Peuterey ridge. If we waited until moonrise we should have plenty of light for this last part of the route to the summit of Mont Blanc.

At about midnight, the whole mountain was flooded with light and shadow. The frost was sharp. It was something of an effort to get moving, but once we had done so it was marvellous. The firm snow squeaked under our crampons and shone with thousands of tiny reflections. By dawn we were more than half-way up the ridge. The horizon hardened, a few plumes were raised from the enchanted summits by the breeze which had begun to freshen. Here were the last rocks. As I climbed on to the summit I was greeted by the most wonderful sight that anyone can see from the top of Mont Blanc; on one side the Italian flank blazing with warmth and light, on the other Savoy still plunged in darkness.

The autumn of 1963 was exceptionally fine, and I was able to do a number of splendid routes ranging from the hitherto unexplored west face of the Trident de Tacul to the south and east faces of the Dent du Géant, from Monte Rosa to the Matterhorn, from the Brenta to Lavaredo and the Sassolungo. Of them all, however, at once the most coveted and unexpected was the first ascent of the east face of the Grand Pilier d'Angle, the forge of the rock falls, on Mont Blanc, the home mountain, on 11–12 October.

It proved a difficult route, mainly on rock, up a series of smooth, vertical, tottery-looking corners and cracks. At night the temperature sank to around $-15°C$ and the snow was everywhere powdery and unstable. So much for the record: but for me the climb represented above all the second half of that symbolic fruit consisting of the Grand Pilier d'Angle.

This ascent raised to nineteen the number of routes I had climbed on the Brenva flank, some of them several times, in summer and in winter. Certain of them have variants, to which others will no doubt be added in the future, but the real routes are and will remain these nineteen: the Peuterey ridge; the north face of the Aiguille Blanche; the north face of the Col de Peuterey; the north and east faces and the north-east spur of the Grand Pilier d'Angle; the Pear buttress; the Route Major; the Sentinelle Rouge; the Old Brenva route; the Diagonal route; the Brenva couloir; the Grüber route; the Giannina route; the Mont Maudit couloir; the Cretier route; the Mont Maudit direct route; the Kagami route; and the Kuffner or frontier ridge.

III

Mountaineering

THE SPORT OF mountaineering was invented a couple of centuries ago by the explorers of the Alps, who, once they had learned the lie of the valleys and passes, felt an urge to conquer the summits. Those strongholds of legend, till then reputed impregnable, fell one after another. Then routes were driven in turn up the ridges, up the faces and buttresses, ever more direct and more difficult. Slowly, what had been natural obstacles to the pioneers became goals for the ardour and tenacity of their descendants. By some, they were taken above all as gauges of their own value in a competition more against themselves than against the mountain, and as a way of expressing man's ancestral dialogue of love with mother nature in terms of action. At this point mountaineering really transcended its origins, assuming an almost philosophical significance. I would say that it acquired a soul, and from there went on to become an active and heroic expression of our age.

God and a man's native land, those supreme and contrasting values which motivated the heroes of the past and to which our contradictory nature still attaches a mystical importance, have lost much of their power in our day. Kings, speeches and mysteries no longer suffice to bring peace and faith. Daily living has become a

round of demands, provocations and doubts. The intel-
lect sweeps away spiritual values even before they are
formed. Deprived of standards in a decadent society
where nothing is fixed or defined, heroism has leaked
away for sheer lack of purpose.

Yet at this very moment the human spirit has produced another heroic movement. Freed from the forms
of orthodoxy upheld by the martyrs and warriors of old,
it has taken a shape more adapted to our times. Its
stimuli have been the frustrations of industrial civiliza-
tion, rebellion against a collectivistic society, a society
almost happy to sink into a general mediocrity, and
always content to seem rather than be. It is also a re-
buttal of disillusion and ignobility and of that security
offered as progress, which, when achieved, makes
spiritual progress impossible. This is why the hero of our
day is against rather than for this flat, tired, "consump-
tive" world, turning his back on it and risking death in
order to escape into the pure solitude of a mountain, an
ocean, a desert.

In comparison with the ancient form of heroism,
always related to some unanimously received and sacred
order, the modern version, as an isolated expression of
individual courage, may appear almost empty, almost
gratuitous. The hero of today may thus indeed seem a
knight of nothingness, a conquistador of the useless,
acting according to his own judgement and circumstances, so that to somebody else he may be absurd and
even unbearable. Yet in this attitude there resides a
persuasive and comforting truth, transcending material-
istic premises and even the pure, intimate satisfaction of

one who lives by it, involved as he sometimes is in the desperate struggle with self, with difficulty, and with widespread lack of understanding. This truth is the truth of man, the face of his dreams of escape, the cry of his flight from social pressures, the nostalgia for a natural condition forgotten but perhaps not yet irrevocably lost, the sign that confirms our human dimension, irreversible and immortal. In every act of courage, consciously or not, it resounds like a hymn to life through the humanity that is shaken out of inaction for a moment.

Knowledge and wisdom are both essential to human progress, but they are not the same thing, as philosophy has long reminded us. However, let us accept our so-called social conquests; let us disembark on the moon and other planets in our insatiable pride; only let us not forget that the destiny of man is to become ever more human. That is what the wise, useless, "mad actions" of our present-day heroes are meant to remind us.

While the foregoing may answer some of the whys of a certain kind of mountaineering, it remains to take a look at standards of difficulty and the means and techniques employed. Obviously the why and the how should be in harmony if the climbing is not to become a phenomenon alien from its significance.

Let us review the stages through which this discipline has passed, starting from the beginning. As the explorers of the Alps began to scale the summits,* they were obliged to invent tools to overcome the difficulties and dangers they encountered. Thus the first rudimentary

* *Translator's note:* In the last quarter of the eighteenth century. The next stage referred to was about the middle of the nineteenth.

climbing-ropes, ice-axes and nailed boots came into being. When the climbers turned to the ridges, rock faces and steep hanging glaciers, these early items of equipment were improved. Crampons for ice and pitons for rock made their appearance. At this stage there was a certain outcry against the use of pitons, some persons considering it a profanation to hammer a piton into rock although they were quite happy to stamp their not strictly indispensable crampons into the ice. One of the leaders of this school was Paul Preuss. Already, therefore, we find ourselves confronted with the convolutions and contradictions of a ripening code of Alpine ethics which was producing its own prophets and disciples. These new-fangled pitons were hammered into natural cracks in the rock, first of all as a means of anchorage, then, as standards of difficulty increased, as an aid to movement. This technique made it possible for the climbers to consider attempting any mountain in the world, and thus extended their field of action. Nevertheless, the peaks still retained the essential fascination of mystery and potential impossibility. The feeling of facing the mountain with equal arms had not been lost; risk and uncertainty, those spurs of the human race, were not eliminated. This period corresponds roughly to the first half of the twentieth century, the golden age of classical mountaineering,* unsurpassable for creativity and the human values that were expressed in it. The

* *Translator's note:* This is a perfectly justifiable opinion of the author's. In order to avoid confusion in the reader's mind, it should perhaps be mentioned that in mountaineering literature "the golden age" generally means the 1860s.

climbers of that period displayed great moral and physical strength, indomitable will-power, conscious audacity, cool reasoning, logic and—not least—a sense of poetry.

The third and present phase of mountaineering is placed under the sign of mechanization, of which many contemporary climbers are protagonists. Among the equipment of these athletes it is not unusual to find genuine builder's tools such as rawlplugs and expansion bolts which can be placed anywhere a hole is drilled in the living rock; drills for this very purpose, whether primitive or power-driven; and a whole box of tricks such as hammocks, transistor radios, pulleys and fixed ropes connecting the climber like an umbilical cord with the foot of the face, whence he can be supplied with his needs and even some extras.

Clearly, when this happens, the mechanic has taken over from the mountaineer. Man has in fact so armed himself as to be able to climb any face whatever with mathematical certainty. Since expansion bolts and all their related paraphernalia began to be used, no over-hang has resisted efforts to climb it. Once again, it is man who has gone under, humiliated by the machine. There is no doubt that this new kind of climbing gives rise to remarkable athletic performances, but the true significance of the sport is lost forever. This automatically brings my summary of heroic mountaineering to a close.

Why is there such devaluation in the works of modern man? Simply because each day brings us a worse example. We care less for the future than for the present, and less still for the past. Paradoxically, mankind has made a new myth of destroying all mythology. Is this a new manifestation of the heroic spirit? I would deny this, but no doubt some will say so. People of this stamp tear down the old myths indiscriminately just to rid themselves of standards. Nowadays, for example, the word "impossible" disturbs and annoys. Perhaps the new generation of climbers has adopted certain techniques precisely to eliminate it from their vocabulary.

As for my own conception of mountaineering, it has been clearly embodied in every climb I have ever done and in my whole way of life. My inspiration has always been in the classical tradition, which suits my temperament and fulfils my requirements. Acting in the line of a tradition built out of sacrifice, suffering and—why not?—love, I have always sought to advance it a little without falsifying its nature, respecting the rule of a game which has a fascination and a justification precisely because the cards have never been stacked in order to win at any cost. It is thus natural that my undertakings have often had the quality of an affirmation of principle against a certain degeneration.

IV

The Walker Spur in Winter

As a result of that evolution which is inseparable from all human activity, the time came when climbers began to think of scaling the highest and most difficult north faces in the Alps at the time of year when the days are shortest, the weather coldest, and the sun never touches the grey armour of ice that covers the rocks. This was to be the most important Alpine development of the 1960s. There are of course innumerable north faces, but three in particular provide a synthesis of their special characteristics. This proud trio consists of the north faces of the Eiger, the Matterhorn and the Grandes Jorasses, high and fascinating mountains which seem created as emblems of grandiose beauty, sheer difficulty, and the very essence of the conquest of the Alps.

The Eigerwand was the first to succumb, being climbed in two stages by a party of four Germans in March 1961. In February the following year two Swiss climbed the Matterhorn north face, an ascent brilliant in its classical purity. Only the northern defences of the Grandes Jorasses, the most difficult and renowned of the three, continued to hold out against all besiegers. Successive failures led many of the latter to conclude that the winter ascent of this face would call for Himalayan techniques, in other words the setting up of several fixed camps, with parties of climbers carrying loads from one to another with the help of pitons and fixed ropes. During the month of March 1962, moreover, this plan was put into operation by four climbers of three different nationalities, but luckily nothing came of it. After four days of work they were still only at grips with the early pitches. Why they gave up I do not know.

For my part, I was firmly of the opinion that the face stood for so much that was pure and ideal that its winter ascent should be approached with respect. And by respect I meant that the difficulties should be faced in the same spirit and conditions as they had been faced by our predecessors, so that their significance would in no way be lessened. What point would there be in climbing a face such as that of the Jorasses at any cost, by virtue of compromises, when the only result would be to rob it of the spell of the unknown, the perhaps impossible, the fight against which commits the whole of our being and revives whatever courage and humanity remain hidden away in us?

Perhaps in the whole story of mountain climbing there has never been such a widespread lack of standards as in recent years. The morals of the rat race are found even among climbers, some of whom go so far as to define their methods as "technical advances" and—perhaps even ingenuously—their dishonest compromises as "progress". The real progress, if any, would be to apply the honourable traditional techniques of Alpine mountaineering to the Himalayas.

I dislike competing with people in the mountains, and up to this time had therefore stood aside from the race for the winter ascents of the great north faces, though longing to measure myself against them. Now, however, I felt such disgust for the growing mediocrity of the sport that I made an inward pledge to vindicate its traditions.

As winter was already over, it was too late to do anything about the matter in 1962, but I was resolved that the following winter would see me on the north face of the Grandes Jorasses. Although the resolve was secret, after the failure of the "Himalayans" my name began to figure mysteriously on the ever-growing list of candidates for the "impossible" north face. Suddenly it was as though there were eyes on me everywhere I went, and I know for a fact that high-speed telephonic messages concerning my movements flashed to and fro between Geneva, Paris, Chamonix, Grindelwald and Munich. The best method of demolishing the opposition is to take it by surprise, so that as autumn came around I began a painstaking but secret programme of physical and psychological preparation. I knew the Walker spur from having climbed it in summer fourteen years earlier, but still more important was the fact that I knew the limits of my own resistance to cold, fatigue and loneliness in the high mountains, which in my opinion is an indispensable basis for the planning of an undertaking of this order. My partner was again to be Cosimo Zappelli, with whom I had built up a good working relationship.

It got into perfect physical shape not by rock-climbing, but mainly by skiing. My friends were astonished to see me suddenly become an assiduous frequenter of the slopes; their surprise was to be even greater when they heard that I was on the north face of the Grandes

Jorasses. The trick worked perfectly. In fact, each time I went up on a cable-car, I descended non-stop in an uninterrupted series of short-radius turns in the worst and deepest snow I could find on some hidden, awkward slope.

Towards Christmas the face seemed to be getting into condition. I set off on the pretext of a ski tour down the Mer de Glace with three friends. At the appropriate point we separated, and while the others skied on down the glacier Zappelli and I plodded up to the so-called Leschaux hut. Up to eight years earlier it had been a comfortable cabin in one of the most magical corners of the Mont Blanc range. Then a monster avalanche had half destroyed it, leaving a few joists and corrugated sheets. Rather than a hut, therefore, it had become a reference point and a place where, by arranging things carefully, it was possible to get some shelter from the wind if not from the snowdrifts that had accumulated inside it.

Unfortunately, the weather broke that evening, and the next day we had to retreat to Chamonix through the thickly falling snow. In order not to draw attention to myself, I was obliged to make my way back to Courmayeur in the most inglorious way possible, on foot through the still uncompleted Mont Blanc tunnel, since the cable-car was not running on account of the bad weather.

A hard, snowy winter set in; the worst in fifty years according to the meteorologists. It was as ill-suited to our project as possible, but now that the cards were down I did not wish to revoke. A month later fine weather

Bonatti climbing an ice-fall.

The Grandes Jorasses and Dent du Géant with the Mer de Glace at their feet.

returned, but the temperature was enough to make a Siberian shiver. Nevertheless, the sun shone, the barometer was high, and the French and Swiss weather bulletins both spoke of settled conditions. On Tuesday, 22 January, I decided to set off the following morning at 7 a.m. Zappelli turned up on the dot, but with a long face, explaining that he could hardly move for pain on account of a dental abscess. And indeed his naturally round face was all swollen out on one side, while his eyes were puffy from a sleepless night. This was a cruel blow. Instead of taking the cable-car up to the Col du Géant we at once drove down to see a dentist in Aosta. However, once the abscess was lanced and some antibiotic taken, a miracle seemed to occur, and by 3 o'clock in the afternoon we were riding up in the cable-car. But high altitude and cold are no palliatives to toothache, and at the Torino hut the trouble started again. How could I go on with a companion in this state? It seemed as though the fates were conspiring against me. After a month and a half spent waiting for the moment to go, hour by hour, everything was falling to pieces. First there had been the unending bad weather, and now this damned business. My temper boiled over. Poor Zappelli sat there suffering, looking at me in despair without saying anything. Like me, however, he had not given up all hope. An hour went by. We could have gone back to our homes for a couple of days, but our now too-numerous rivals would certainly get in our hair. What should we do? Suddenly, by some happy impulse, we snapped on our skis and headed down the Mer de Glace.

F

The sun was setting. Before us, like a funeral pyre, the Dru shone red, while the wind-blown lower ridges smoked in the violet sky. The silence was brooding and full of tension. Perhaps next day we should have to trudge back up these snow-slopes down which we were now whizzing. As we reached the great curve of the Mer de Glace we bore off to the right and began to ascend the Leschaux glacier in the grey twilight. The cold became more and more biting. At almost regular intervals, Zappelli had attacks of violent pain in his jaw. Like robots we went on, refusing to think of retreat. By the time we reached the remains of the hut it was totally dark. A month earlier we had hidden some equipment here which we now unearthed by the light of our headtorches. Next came the rite of preparing the sacks. How much and what kind of provisions should we take? How long would the adventure last? In view of the uncertainty, we allowed for reserves of everything, with the result that the sacks became so heavy that we could not hope to reach the foot of the face in one day. Silently and hastily we gobbled a snack, then sorted out our bivouac. A few tranquillizer pills made it possible for Zappelli to get to sleep.

Next morning, 24 January, we rose before dawn. The sky was still starry, and the thermometer showed a temperature of −20°C. Once again, everything depended on the condition of my companion. He seemed more recovered than I had dared to hope. Without wasting time we shouldered our sacks, clipped on our skis, and headed towards the face. As the sky paled we began to see our mountain face-on for the first time in a month.

In the steely light the sharp, commanding outlines of the north face seemed symbolic of all that was inaccessible, a worthy throne for a god.

For a couple of hours we marched onwards, the weight of our sacks becoming ever more crushing. On the flat glacier the snow was crusty and deep. As the angle began to steepen, our shoulders began to feel as though they were breaking. We therefore divided the loads into two, leaving half in a conspicuous position and continuing with the rest. With the more human loads the work was less exhausting. We would carry for an hour and a half, dump the sacks, and return for the last lot. Towards 1 o'clock we decided to have a bite to eat. The meat was frozen to stone, but we just ate it all the same. Our halt seemed the cue for a wind to sweep down the glacier, raising clouds of ice particles. We kept up our shuttle service, sinking deeper and deeper into the snow, which had become difficult and tiresome. The crust had to be broken at every step before one could move forward over the ski. As we thus trudged along we instinctively looked around us; it seemed impossible that we should be alone on the way to attack the most grandiose and coveted of all the great climbs in the world, yet there was not a soul to be seen. Whereas the evening before we had noticed tracks leading to the Leschaux hut, now we saw not a sign of one the whole day long.

Towards dusk we reached the foot of the face. Our surroundings seemed to me all the more beautiful because we had succeeded in carrying up our loads and because Zappelli was now definitely cured. We therefore levelled a few square metres of snow in the shelter of a big sérac and settled down to what may as well be called our second bivouac on the approach march. Though night was falling and we were tired, this did not prevent us from making a reconnaissance up to the rimaye in order to check the conditions. The start was one steep boilerplate of emerald-green ice which looked as though it would call for a lot of time and effort. Just to see, we climbed up a few metres. It proved impossible to move a step without chipping away a notch in which to place the front points of our crampons.

The sun set and darkness fell without any transition, surprising us where we stood gazing up at that pitiless mountain wall, 1,280 metres high, already of extreme difficulty in summer and absolutely unknown in winter conditions. Every one of those metres held unforeseeable and perhaps insurmountable difficulties. An ascent of this kind takes several days, which increases the risk of bad weather. On the other side of the scale, I was re-assured by awareness of our careful preparation. Never-theless, I hoped devoutly for that little bit of good luck which is indispensable in any hazardous enterprise. Even if I looked away, I could still feel the face weighing down on me. I caught myself questioning it, telling it my hopes, as though it were a living creature. And as it showed its opaque, frozen profile through the night, it seemed to be replying; an immeasurable, impassive ice-sphinx.

We clambered down to our little snow platform and settled down to a disturbed, interminable bivouac. At first we dozed fitfully, but towards midnight a steady, bitterly cold wind sprang up, and from then on we lay

Bonatti on skis heading for the foot of the north face of the Grandes Jorasses (24 January 1963).

The grandiose north face of the Grandes Jorasses.

Mont Blanc by moonlight seen from the ordinary route on the Grandes Jorasses.

awake wearily waiting for dawn. We were stirring even before daybreak, this being the only way to obtain any relief from the torture.

As the sky began to pale we were putting the finishing touches to our preparations. Our rucksacks contained what we might need immediately; the rest was packed into a big, cylindrical, canvas bag designed to be hauled up after us pitch by pitch. At 8.30 a.m. on 25 January 1963 we put on the rope, and the attack on the great north face began.

Planting the first belay piton, I started the heavy labour of cutting steps up the ice-slope. This took over an hour. I felt ill at ease, partly because of the cold which inhibited my movements, partly because this same cold rendered the ice excessively brittle. At each stroke of the axe it would shatter like a pane of glass with cracks spreading in all directions, so that I had to make certain that each step was not flawed before I put my weight on it. Thus I ran out 40 metres of rope, climbing diagonally and gradually gaining in co-ordination and confidence. For a moment even the mountain seemed to smile, a small yellow facet of the summit standing bathed in sunlight. Before moving up to join me, Zappelli, as agreed, let go the cylindrical sack, which swung pendulum-like in space. Standing balanced between rock and ice, I hauled it slowly upwards, a manœuvre that was to be repeated innumerable times during the day. I said nothing to my companion. We communicated in monosyllables, seeking to eliminate every superfluous gesture and expression.

The wind had dropped. The clarity of the icy blue

shadow in which we stood was tangible, ringing, pure and remote. The cold was arctic, the air like chilled metal. Because I was now scrambling up a kind of plinth of relatively easy-angled, glazed rock I was able to keep my gloves on for the time being, but I knew that before long I should have to take them off and climb with bare hands. The hours slipped by without our noticing, and our almost monotonous progress made us forget hunger and thirst.

Suddenly the sepulchral silence of the mountains was broken by the far-off throbbing of a motor. Shortly afterwards a tiny speck appeared against the sky above Chamonix, scintillating in the sunlight. Soon it became recognizable as a helicopter heading straight for us. I remembered that our friend Mario De Biasi had said that on the third day he would come and see how we were getting on. He had kept his promise. After a few sinuous manœuvres to get the feel of the air currents, the fragile steel dragon-fly came closer and closer until it was hovering only two or three score metres away from us. In the plexiglas bubble we could recognize our friend waving to us. We were overcome with emotion. The tears poured down Zappelli's cheeks and I could hardly restrain my own. This face-to-face encounter with De Biasi, impossible yet real, recalled us to the facts of our situation, how isolated we were from any form of life, how unattainable it was even though floating in the air a few metres away. Our initial joy swiftly gave way to an attack of loneliness.

The helicopter moved away and faded into the distance. Absolute silence returned. We continued to climb, but I was aware that my gaze returned more often than before to those four bits of wood, our skis, stuck upright into the snow at the foot of the face, which together with ourselves were the only things alien to the pitiless, indifferent world around us. Of the three great north faces, that of the Jorasses has the peculiarity of being so situated that the climber never sees any sign of life even on the farthest horizon. There is no sound but those of the gale, the avalanche and the thunder. Anyone who climbs it in winter might well imagine himself in the wastes of the Antarctic or on a lifeless planet.

Meanwhile we had reached the edge of the great ice-slope. The sack was becoming an obsession. The continual rubbing against the rock was beginning to lacerate it, and I was afraid it might not last out the climb.

Towards evening I thought I heard the croaking of a raven, but somehow it seemed too far-fetched in a place so utterly hostile to life. However, it turned out to be real, and even seemed to appreciate our company. Black, furtive, erratic, it soared in its element, the smooth wind-currents. With a sudden clap of its wings it would drop off the up-draught into a whistling dive, then ride it back up again, playing with a lyrical casualness, following the eddies of air. Sometimes it would hover motionless as though it had perched on the sky, then suddenly it would begin to describe parabolas, rolls and gyres of striking elegance. It would dart in exultation and glide in an ecstasy of silent flight, its wings tense and open. Now and again it would utter a harsh, sonorous cry, and in the ensuing silence seemed to be enjoying the echoes. As it glided around the contours of the face it sometimes almost brushed me in passing, but mostly the black form appeared swift and piratical against the bright background of glacier, or superbly etched on the blue dome of the sky. They say that the raven is a bird of ill-omen, but I do not believe it. In those surroundings its presence was infinitely friendly and comforting.

The light faded rapidly and the night engulfed us while still looking for a good bivouac site. I kept on searching, however, and finally, in total darkness, succeeded in planting a safe piton above a couple of narrow bulges which, when cleared of ice, would serve as resting-places. We were now at approximately 3,200 metres. With our legs swinging in space we sat down and cocooned ourselves in loops of rope attached to the piton. The weather hardly seemed worth a thought; the sky was starry and the cold as sidereal as ever. Although the smallest movements were complicated, we succeeded in lighting our gas cooker and making a drink which we swallowed while still no more than mildly warm in order to save gas.

At dawn on Saturday the barometer had gone down a few millimetres. Quite soon a fine mother-of-pearl veil drifted southwards across the sky. The wind direction was was still favourable, and I reckoned that any bad weather would be short-lived. This proved to be a mistake. Getting ready for action took longer than expected, and we did not start climbing until 9.30 a.m. Some 70 metres above us loomed the first major difficulty, the Allain crack. Contrary to our expectations, however, on this particular day we were destined to do no more than see it. Towards midday the increasingly compact cloud-layer began to be torn by the claws of the storm. Soon we were in the midst of a genuine blizzard, blocked on a small ledge before even reaching the difficulties.

The shrieking wind whirled up the snow with such violence that it was impossible to keep our eyes open. It penetrated everywhere, including the supposedly airtight bivouac sack. Knowing that we should give up, I was overcome by a profound feeling of discouragement. The afternoon dragged by, and still I could not find the courage to take this decision. As night fell the wind only grew stronger and more furious. Despite urgent calls of nature, the snow drove so fiercely that we dared not open the sack. We therefore held out all night, and in the morning the operation caused us major discomfort.

Dawn on Sunday brought continued snow-squalls, roaring wind and a struggling, dismal light. In view of the continuing bad weather the sensible course would have been to retreat, but somehow this ascent had cost me too much worry and sacrifice, and I could not resign myself to this tame conclusion. Our excellent bivouac equipment made it possible to postpone the painful decision for another 24 hours. To cover up my depression, I said flippantly: "Why should we climb down today, anyway? It's Sunday."

At dawn the temperature was −30°C, but in the early afternoon it unexpectedly became warmer. The wind fell, and by evening the barometer had risen five millimetres. The certainty of being able to continue the climb cheered us, and after greeting our friend the raven, who had resumed his tours of inspection, we prepared for our third bivouac in good heart.

The fourth dawn found us still only at 3,300 metres.

We had been moored to the same piton for more than 43 hours. During the night, however, I had been mulling over a decision which was to prove important for the success of our undertaking. We were on excellent form, and the haulage sack, despite the desirability of its contents, was holding us up too much. After taking out food for three days, therefore, we would leave it secured to a piton. It was as though we had contracted a term of expiry with ourselves. Within this brief period the remaining 900 metres of face would have to be overcome. If the barometer was anything to go by, we could expect a few days of fine weather. The greatly reduced total weight would favour more rapid climbing even if our actual rucksacks would henceforward be heavier.

We were ready to go by 8 o'clock. Right at the outset the Allain crack sorely tested my muscles, which had grown stiff in the course of almost two days of forced idleness. The first contact with the rock and with the iron of the pitons was like putting my hands into flame, first scorching the skin, then robbing the fingers of strength. In the excitement of the moment, Zappelli inadvertently held a piton between his lips. By the time he remembered and snatched it away, the damage was done and the lips were swollen and bleeding. On faces like this, in winter, normally insignificant gestures may have unforeseeable consequences, and all the more so during a spell of exceptional cold such as we were undergoing. On our return, I was to read in the newspapers for this day that a polar air-current was covering Europe. Even in the plains of northern Italy a temperature of $-25°C$ was recorded.

Though the Allain crack is only 30 metres high, it took me over two hours to climb it. The rock was smooth and overhanging, the cracks so choked with ice that it was difficult to hammer in pitons. The weight of the sack dragged outwards; my numbed hands had almost no feeling left in them. Hampered as we were with equipment and winter outfits, our movements were clumsy, and below us yawned a void of over 300 metres.

Once this crucial pitch had been overcome we began to feel better. The next problem was a long stretch of bare ice which cost me some hard step-cutting, but this had the advantage of warming and loosening me up. By 11.30 a.m. we stood at the foot of the second major difficulty, the 90 metre corner. It was in curious condition, areas of bare rock alternating with incrustations of treacherous snow sticking even to overhangs. By luck, on the line I had to follow there was relatively little clearing to be done to find the cracks and holds. Most of the time, by bridging widely, it was possible to avoid these patches. It was acrobatic and exposed, but rapid and elegant, and in this way we reached the top of the corner in only two hours.

We now had to find our way up smooth slabs almost constantly overlaid with ice, but we were going so well and our morale was such that we no longer felt the cold or the weight of the sacks. It did not even occur to us to feel hungry or notice that we had hardly slept for five days. The weather was more radiant than ever, we had attained a state of grace, and for the first time I felt the conviction that we were going to succeed.

At 4 o'clock in the afternoon we were at 3,600 metres,

below the pendulum abseil which is the turning-point of the ascent. Here the way ahead is barred by a smooth, overhanging wall, and it is necessary to descend 10 metres or so on a rope suspended from a convenient piton. Then, still hanging on to the rope, you begin to swing, and, after acquiring momentum, run across to the right, perpendicular to the rock as though freed from gravity but in fact still pivoting on the rope, until some holds are reached at full stretch and used to haul across on to a small ledge. When I had completed this manœuvre, my companion joined me with the help of the rope which linked us together. Next the abseil rope was pulled down from the piton. This is a solemn moment, since tradition has it that henceforward all possibility of retreat is cut off. Our bridges were therefore burnt; we were committed. But by now we were at such voltage that we felt as though we were being fired up the rocks. Our morale was set fair.

After flaming for a time on the peaks opposite, the sun was slowly dying like a spent candle, but we kept on climbing. Forty metres higher up we found a large flake. After hacking it clear of its coating of ice we installed ourselves side by side, half upright and still roped up. The first shadows of the night began to darken the violet pallor of the horizon, welling out of the valleys like dark water gradually submerging the world. The first stars seemed to loiter, then suddenly shone out in a cobalt sky.

We crouched face outwards. It was impossible to move an inch. Above us hulked the obscure mass of the terrible and notorious black slabs. Another day had gone

The north face of the Grandes Jorasses:
——————— The Walker spur (first winter ascent by Bonatti and
Zappelli, 25–30 January 1963)
- - - - - - the Whymper spur (first ascent by Bonatti and Vaucher,
6–9 August 1964)
O   Bivouacs

Bonatti during training prior to the winter ascent of the Walker spur.

by; another night, our sixth, had fallen. We ate some smoked bacon, biscuits and a little dried fruit. I wedged the cooker behind a flake, sheltering it from the wind with one arm. Over the weak flame I melted a few handfuls of snow which, mixed with a little sugar, would constitute our best restorative. Every so often I had to hug the cylinder to my chest, under my outer clothing, in order to prevent the cold slowly freezing the gas.

In the course of the climb I often thought of my earlier ascent in summer. I had been nineteen years old, and the combined ages of myself and my partner, Andrea Oggioni, barely added up to thirty-eight. We were a pair of unknown boys, and we had ventured to pit ourselves against what was reputed to be the hardest of all mountain faces. Before us only five parties of famous mountaineers had climbed it, starting with Cassin, Esposito and Tizzoni in 1938. I remember those days as the most intense of my life up to then, and as the most glorious and exalting act available to me in my total poverty. Indeed, both of us were so poor that neither of us possessed even a balaclava; we had to make do with a scarf or with a cotton shopping-bag with holes cut in it for the eyes. The sacks and clothing were army surplus, the rope a worn length of hemp, the pitons sawn out of an iron bar, and our nourishment half a dozen apples bought on credit. Nevertheless, we were the happiest boys in the world, and the richest too in our will to live. When all is said and done, one does not need much to be able to smile at life.

So now, fourteen years later, we were in good humour, cracking jokes until drowsiness overcame us. Dozing fitfully, I several times had the impression of sliding, but as is the way in dreams nothing happened. The hours went by. Zappelli slept. Suddenly, a yell. I awoke with a start, hanging on the rope. My dream had been translated into reality, and I had slithered on the ice, fetching up in a heap a metre lower down. Finally I settled down in this new position.

Glancing around at the horizon, I noticed that a great black blotch had blanked off the stars above the Aiguille Verte. I checked the barometer: it was sinking slowly. The weather was playing us tricks again. The hours that remained until dawn crawled by in anxiety. Would we succeed in climbing the second half of the face before the storm arrived?

Next day was Tuesday. The light of dawn found us already attached to the overhangs of the black slabs. That morning, more than all others, our skis abandoned at the foot of the face seemed frail and unattainable. Long black clouds were voyaging out across the sky from the north-east, a sign of coming storm. It was heralded by a tremendous wind that hindered us greatly. The moment had come to play for the ultimate stakes. The difficulties were sustained. In order to climb as quickly as possible I was obliged to take off my gloves and place very few pitons for security. It was almost all free climbing, and I was utterly reliant on my hands. It grew colder and colder. The light waned to a kind of faded whiteness mixed with tones of misty grey. As in flight from an enemy, nothing could be allowed to hold up our race towards the summit.

Thus we hastened up the black slabs and the steep

rocks above, the central hogsback ridge, and the red chimney, hardly noticing the icy, flaming sunset. The blizzard was now at our heels. Gusts of snow powder whirled chokingly around us, and the thermometer I was carrying around my neck reached its lower limit of −35°C, or it would probably have gone lower. If we stopped, we should be paralysed. Fear showed on our faces. It was a matter of life and death to get the last remaining difficulties behind us that same evening, even if it cost us a bivouac suspended from a piton. If night and the freezing storm blocked us below those final obstacles, it would be the end.

At an altitude of 4,050 metres we struggled across the horizontal traverse below the red tower and up the over-hanging chimney which follows. The last light was gone out of the world. Around him, each of us could see nothing but the white line of rope that linked him to the other. I hammered in a piton, attached the rope to it, then slid back down to Zappelli, who was suffering torture from the cold during his enforced wait. Without more ado we anchored ourselves to the rope and climbed into the bivouac sack which, however, seemed to have lost all heat-preserving qualities under the effect of the freezing squalls.

The blizzard now rose to a climax, battering us from side to side. Our feet, hanging in space, quickly lost all feeling. The humidity in our breath condensed instantly, building up a crust of ice on our faces. We passed the time beating our feet and rubbing various parts of our bodies as they started going numb. To fall asleep in these conditions would mean never waking up again.

Our anxiety was such that we did not have the courage to discuss our situation. How helpless man is before the forces of nature, yet how great in his helplessness! Sometimes, as I closed my eyes, I had the impression of being in a storm at sea. The heavy squalls would burst against the frozen rock-wall with a roar like a wave, the spray from which turned into thousands of stinging ice-needles. Then I would have the feeling of being a ship-wrecked mariner, with the slender line that secured us to the piton as our life-raft.

That night was never-ending. When dawn came at last it was livid and opaque. The Leschaux glacier was hidden by a dense sea of cloud. Above, a leaden cowl hung oppressively over the mountain. Now and again the Aiguille Verte and the Dru would half show through for a moment like distant ghosts. Only 130 metres separated us from the summit, but it seemed quite unattainable. What would have become of us if we had not reached this point the day before? Wearily we set about climbing again. The gale was still roaring against the crags, cracking away plates of ice. There were times when hands and feet simply seemed to be refusing to do their job. Somehow I had to get up this last stretch, however. I was determined to get there; determined to survive. It was at this moment that the will revealed itself stronger than the unchained elements. My hands no longer caressed the icy holds: they gripped them like vices. This was no Sunday-afternoon pleasure climb, but a desperate struggle for survival.

The summital snow cornice became visible looming above us. Another 30 metres of ice-glazed rock, then a

Amid storms, overhangs and virgin snow: Bonatti in training for the assault on the north face of the Grandes Jorasses in winter.

Zappelli belaying Bonatti across a traverse near the Allain crack on the Walker spur.

smooth granite slab thickly fringed with frost-rime. The skin of my hands was sticking to the rock. Clenching my teeth with the pain, I made one more acrobatic struggle upwards, ending under the gigantic, spectral roll of snow. It was like a vision seen between sleep and waking. At the left end showed a dull greenish translucency; I started trying to break through at this point, but found myself blinded by a spray of ice-dust. With my eyes practically shut, the lids crusted with ice, I lifted the axe and planted it on the other side of the crest. A moment later I was rolling in the snow on the summit of the Grandes Jorasses.

I stood up, only to be blown away by the hurricane. After staggering a few paces I got my balance back; it took time to understand that there was nothing to hold on to with my hands. To experience two such different realities in the space of a minute is almost impossible to grasp. In front of me lay liberation from the harassing anxieties with which we had lived uninterruptedly for seven days; behind, the nightmare still existed. I could not see my companion as he struggled up towards me, but I could imagine every gesture, his face packed round with snow, the grabbing at the last ice-coated holds, the frenzied haste to have done with it all as though fleeing from a monster snapping at his heels, and above all the desire to see over the other side, towards the diffused light that rose out of Italy. He was thirsty for light, for horizontal lines, sights warm with affection and memory. His physical hunger would be forgotten in the supreme desire to be finished with it all. A minute earlier I had been in exactly the same state.

And at last there he was, clambering over the snow-fringe of the summit. Our eyes met: we threw our arms around one another in exultation. For a moment the tension even went out of the rope. The bond which had stretched taut between us all up the face now dropped in a disorderly pile at our feet. All this lasted a few seconds. Then we again noticed the paralysing cold, the wind blowing the words back down our throats, the snow-laden gusts lashing our faces. I wanted to record this moment of life in a place where life could not exist, so we snapped photographs of one another with the camera that had become a lump of ice. Who knew whether we should succeed in preserving this vision?

We began to stagger downhill. I glanced at my watch: it was almost 10 a.m. Sometimes the valley could be half glimpsed through the whirling snow. New worries began to replace those that had racked us for the last few days. It was no longer a question of verticality, smooth rock, or the danger of getting stuck on the face. Now it was the menace of avalanches and of innocent-looking snow-slopes that might open under our feet or turn into a maze where we might lose ourselves in the blizzard and disappear forever.

As we made our way down the summital dome of the Grandes Jorasses the grinding of our crampons on bare ice began to be audible above the din of the ever less clamorous gale. Then the ice gave way to snow-cloaked rock, which, however, proved no great problem. Crossing the Whymper gave me some food for thought, but the redoubted avalanche did not occur. It was still snowing abundantly, and I was afraid of another bivouac

in the storm. As we reached the Reposoir* I had a bright
idea: two abseils down the side-wall of the buttress and
we should be able to run straight down the glacier.
When we reached it, however, the snow was exhaustingly
deep and the visibility poor. In order to break a trail
through it we wallowed along, sinking in up to the waist
and leaving a deep trench behind us. Nevertheless, we
lost height steadily, and as we descended the frost re-
lented so that we began to feel the weight of our clothing.
The thermometer still showed $-15°$C. As I eased off my
down jacket I began to wonder how long I had had it on.
When had I donned it? Seven days earlier, about 3
o'clock in the afternoon, on the cable-car taking us up
to the Torino hut.

We did not stop at the Grandes Jorasses hut; in fact
we did not even go over to it, but just went straight on
down the avalanche grooves to the floor of the Val
Ferret. I took it for granted that somebody would be
there waiting for us, but in the event there was not a
trace of human life to be seen. The snow was virgin as it
had been on the Glacier des Grandes Jorasses. I could
not restrain an oath. It was now 5 o'clock in the afternoon and not yet dark. To cover the next few kilometres
of flat ground, where a tarred road lay under the snow,
took us about three hours. It seemed ridiculous! But
the final farce had not yet even begun. As we entered the
first bar in Entrèves, the last outpost of humanity before
what in winter might as well be the wilderness, people
started up in surprise and asked us: "But weren't you

* *Translator's note:* The flat top of a long rib of easy rock on the
ordinary route of the Grandes Jorasses.

supposed to get here tomorrow?" As I saw the television in the corner I understood. On the screen a mountaineering notability was in the process of explaining gravely that if all went well Zappelli and I might reach the summit next day.

I called a taxi to take me home. Incredibly enough, no one was waiting for me there either, so I settled down for an hour outside the front door. It was my eighth bivouac.

V

In the Lap of Zeus

As I WALKED off the ship at Piraeus in May 1963 it was pouring with rain. Thunder rolled echoing down city streets transformed into rushing torrents that reflected the sinister gleam of lightning. And this in a city which claims to get only a dozen or so days of bad weather per year!

I had come to Greece to climb Parnassus and Olympus, the sacred mountains of Hellenic mythology, and the storm seemed ominously like an expression of displeasure on the part of some offended divinity. It pleased me to have something to attribute to the gods already, although I had only just set foot on Greek soil.

The next ten days were spent playing the tourist among the fascinating monuments of ancient Greece. By the time I reached Delphi, my starting-point for Parnassus, I had almost begun to identify with the pilgrims of an earlier age, who nourished so great a respect for the sacred precincts of Phoebus Apollo that before any visit they underwent purificatory ablutions in the Castalian spring, feelings that I understood and shared. It seemed that I had entered into communion with the spirit of those far-off times, always oriented towards immortality, beauty and poetry.

To one in this state of mind, the ascents of Parnassus

and Olympus could not but prove unforgettable and
deeply suggestive. It was like a parenthesis in my existence, an interlude in another world, spent in close
rapport with its inhabitants at once human and divine.
It was as though I were being shadowed and protected;
I felt that each act, each thought, was being weighed
and, as occasion might demand, criticized. The sounds
of nature interwove themselves with dreams and remembered images, and it pleased me to remember them
as the voices of Zeus, Hermes, Aeolus, Pallas, Poseidon,
Hades and Hephaestus, gathered on these lonely mountains from their realms of the heavens, the sea and the
underworld in high dispute over their problems and those
of the world. In a moment of rapture on the slopes of
Parnassus, I picked a small red anemone to lay as
tribute to the Muses on the summit, swept by a raging
squall of hail as I reached it. For me this pagan gesture
was intended as an act of homage to the glorious past of
humanity, the spirit which survives like an inspiring
legend in the reality of those mountains.

Situated between the Boeotian plain and the northern
shore of the Gulf of Corinth, Parnassus, unlike Olympus,
presents no climbing difficulties as such. The highest
summit, which has an altitude of 2,458 metres, was
already climbed in ancient times, and is rounded with
scree-covered sides. There are only a few small cliffs.
Nevertheless, the bleak, austere grandeur of the landscape and the fact that it was sacred to the Muses and
Phoebus, whose oracle at Delphi made of it "the navel
of the world", render it one of the most magical places I
have ever visited.

The range of Olympus extends over a surface area of some 2,000 square kilometres on the western side of the Gulf of Thermai. At 2,917 metres it is the highest mountain in Greece, and its summit, the Mytikas or Pantheon, is no more than 18 kilometres from the sea. Next in height, and moving southwards, come Skolio (2,911 m); Stefàni (2,909 m), also known as the Throne of Zeus; and Skala (2,866 m). These summits represent the central chain of the whole massif. They are pointed limestone peaks with vertical walls which on the western side are up to 500 metres high. Divided by ample scree basins, the minor peaks form a corona around them, more rounded in shape but always solemnly impressive in their vastness and barrenness.

This lower part of the Olympus range, below an altitude of 1,500 metres, is varied and complex in its relief. Innumerable chains extend outwards from the central knot of mountains, often divided by precipitous gorges full of dense vegetation. The stands of timber are mostly pine and spruce, but also beech. On the lower slopes oak and other deciduous varieties abound, together with richly scented flowers such as the Olympus orchid. Among the woods and ravines live wolves, foxes, jackals, wild boar, hare and roe deer. The formerly numerous red deer and bears have now died out.

The rugged architecture of the higher Olympian peaks, especially Mytikas and the Throne of Zeus, gives rise to almost constant turbulence and cloud, which frequently discharge in storm. No clearer motive could be found for the Hellenes' attribution of their highest mysteries to these regions. For them it was nothing less than the royal dwelling of the supreme divinity, from which Zeus, creator of human destiny, dispatched blessings, thunderbolts and death to the world and to mankind. In their turn, supplicants climbed up twice a year to a place within sight of his throne, an easy summit nowadays known as Profitis Ilias, where there was an altar on which to offer sacrifices.

As the centuries went by, changes in population and religion left Olympus shorn of its divinity. It returned to being an ordinary mountain, too rugged to offer anything but pasture for flocks, a refuge to men on the run, and a place where monks could meditate in isolation. Those of the great monastery of Aghios Dionysios were noted for holding religious ceremonies on the summit of Profitis Ilias where St Dionysius built a chapel in the twelfth century over the ruins of the old pagan altar.

At the beginning of the nineteenth century there was a stirring of interest in the exploration of this great mountain which had lain for so long in oblivion. The first to arrive were geologists, surveyors and naturalists, but the presence of brigands made it unsafe to stop for long, thus rendering their studies practically impossible. Not until a few decades later did Olympus return to public notice, and then owing to the advent of mountaineers, who found a unique and pleasing blend of legend and reality upon those myth-hallowed summits.

The first phase in the mountaineering history of Olympus began in 1856, when the French archaeologist L. Heuzey reached the summit of Profitis Ilias, which he mistakenly supposed to be the highest in the range. In 1862 it was the turn of Skolio to be climbed by the

German geographer Heinrich Barth. Setting out from Kokkinoplòs, the latter also made the first ascent of the outlying summit Aghios Antonios (2,815 m) and descended to Litòchoron.

A different kind of adventure occurred to another German geographer called Eduard Richter, who set out from Kokkinoplòs in May 1911 with two companions. After a couple of hours they were captured by brigands and held prisoner for three months until a considerable ransom had been paid. At this time the Balkan wars were still going on, but when the fighting was over, two Swiss, Fred Boissonnas and Daniel Baud-Bovy, rolled up at Litòchoron, engaged the local guide Kakalòs and, on 2 August 1912, succeeded in traversing Skala to the hitherto unclimbed Mytikas, the highest point in the range. The conquest of the last virgin summit fell to the well-known Swiss engineer, cartographer and mountaineer Marcel Kurz in August 1921. He was accompanied by Kakalòs, who thus became an expert on the massif.

Nowadays quite a lot of climbers of all standards visit Olympus during the summer months. Although some problems remain to be solved, the period of exploration is drawing to a close as in the Alps. The usual worried question is being asked: Now that the first ascents have all been done, what will remain to interest future generations? I seem to glimpse the most hopeful answer in an account by the Greek writer Ilias Venezis of an ascent which he made years ago with the American Francis Farquhar.

Farquhar had been among the first to try to reach the highest summit of Olympus. He thought he had succeeded in 1914, but it turned out that there was a point 12 metres higher than the one he had reached, and Boissonnas and Bovy got in before him. But Olympus continued to call him back. Forty years later, their hearts full of pain at the loss of their son, he and his wife left far-off California and returned to Greece to climb the mountain again, including the 12 metres that had escaped him on the earlier occasion. But was this the real reason for his journey? From the door of the Olympus climbing hut, Venezis and Farquhar stood looking up at Mytikas and the Throne of Zeus, which they were to climb next day. "Why have you returned to Olympus at this time of mourning?" asked the former. "Did you come on account of the 12 metres? Or was it to forget?" There was no reply. Venezis turned to look at his companion, a tough man who had been to the North Pole and climbed in the Himalaya, and saw that he was crying. Venezis was embarrassed and begged his pardon. "No," said Farquhar, "I am sorry for not being able to control myself. The answer to your question is that I have come in order to feel the inner peace of simple folk among these beautiful surroundings, in order to understand, in order to see the meaning of our destiny. Not to forget, but to understand." As he spoke he had been gazing at the bare crags above. He glanced down and saw the book that Venezis was holding. "Read me a few lines," he asked. And at the foot of the Throne of Zeus, Venezis read him the opening verses of the *Iliad*.

VI

The North Face of the Eiger

I HAD BEGUN climbing at 5 o'clock in the morning, and by 8.30 a.m. 800 metres of the tremendous north wall of the Eiger lay below me. I had climbed the broken pillar, the difficult crack and the Hinterstoisser traverse, now devalued with a fixed rope, and had reached the placeknown as the Swallow's Nest, an airy ledge sheltered by a bulge of rock and thus an ideal bivouac site. Some party had left a stack of pitons and a sack full of food and other equipment, clear witness that they had decided to reduce their time on the face and go through in two days. Notwithstanding the heavy rucksack which hung from my shoulders, my progress up to this point had been rapid and safe. After a week of persistently bad weather, my morale was again high. It was 28 July 1963.

While recognizing the importance of the Eigerwand, I had never cared for it. Of the famous trio of north faces it is not the hardest, but unquestionably the most dangerous on account of the frequent stonefall. Uncontrolled risk as an end in itself has never attracted me, and I must admit that I have always nourished a kind of preventive instinct for this particular mountain although I have done much more dangerous ones and even have a leaning towards complicated faces of mixed rock and ice. However, here I was, all on my own, obedient to the mysterious lure of the trio. Solitude was my chosen weapon for the symbolic battle with the Ogre.

The history of this face is terrible and marvellous as the odysseys of those who fought on it in pursuit of an ideal and did not come back. There are dozens of names. Practically every feature of the face is associated with some tragedy, and in some cases the dramas have given names to the features as in the case of the Hinterstoisser traverse or the death bivouac. The main causes of these tragedies, the more disconcerting in that most of the protagonists were highly competent, have been stonefall and storm, which, on a wall of such proportions—it is 1,800 metres high—can render retreat problematic. In the Oberland, as on Mont Blanc, bad weather can arrive very suddenly, because these mountains are the vanguard which unfavourable air-currents from the Atlantic strike first. Another cause of trouble in the past was a mistaken evaluation of the type of climbing. Unlike other north faces in the high Alps, the Eigerwand does not rise out of a glacier but almost without warning from the flowery pastures above the Kleine Schiedegg. Its summit, however, just about brushes 4,000 metres, an altitude which constitutes a warning in itself. Those who first attempted the face took it to be simply a structure of smooth, vertical, loose limestone cliffs, which is how it looks from below. It took time for the fact to sink in that it is really a severe and complicated mixture of rock and ice. More than anything else, it is a monstrous funnel of black, glassy ice of the most redoubtable kind, inexhaustibly supplied during thaw weather by the numerous high-altitude snowfields hidden all over it.

Towards 1935, as attempts on the face became more frequent, a veritable carnage began. The victims were climbers of outstanding ability on pure rock, but ill-prepared for the treacherous conditions of high mountains. Several years were to pass before the very powerful team of Heckmair and Vörg from Munich and Kasparek and Harrer from Vienna, attacking separately and later joining forces, succeeded in solving the problem. This took place between 21 and 24 July 1938, a great date in the history of mountaineering. To repeat the face, now a legend of combat, competition, heroism and glory, also called for a great deal of courage. This feat was accomplished by the outstanding French team of Terray and Lachenal who, in three days during July 1947, challenged and vanquished the implacable Ogre.

From then on ascents became more frequent. The Eigerwand ceased to be psychologically "impossible". Its nature and reactions came to be better known, like those of a wild beast in the process of being tamed. Its difficulties and dangers became almost a familiar matter, and the same was true even of the tragedies which, however, continued to occur from time to time. By contrast with the earlier period, it was now the custom to ascribe these more to human misjudgement than to the mountain. If originally success on the Eigerwand was reserved to meticulously prepared parties, it now came to pass that, through a natural process of psychological depreciation which occurs with all climbs of this character, demonstrations of ignorance and unpreparedness became ever more frequent. Some paid for this with their lives, but in fact the most amazing thing was how some hare-brained adventures failed to end in tragedy. I do not say that everyone should try to race up the climb in a day, although this would certainly be the best tactic, but some parties have spent up to a week ambling gently up the face, bivouacking more or less anywhere there was an acute risk of stonefall, icefall, avalanches and bad weather, and yet emerged unscathed on the summit.

I was not the first man to tackle the Eigerwand alone. Two others had tried in recent years, but both had died in the attempt. The aura of fatality and blood that hangs over this killer mountain seemed painfully distinct to the eyes of a solo climber, restoring to it the atmosphere of the early ascents.

I appeared on the first snowfield simultaneously with the first thundering salvo of boulders, and I just had time to dodge smartly back into the Swallows' Nest before they came hooting by. The incident did not surprise me; it is natural on a face like this that as soon as the upper snow-slopes are touched by the sun they should start to unload their wares, especially after a few days of bad weather, and it was by chance that with the whole wide face available they had fallen exactly where I happened to be. No harm had been done. I therefore started again up the first snowfield, which in fact consisted of bare ice. Above it came a difficult, glazed chimney known as the ice-hose, then the second snowfield, up which I began to nick steps. Unfortunately it was a particularly sultry morning, and my step-cutting was carried out to a counterpoint of echoing stonefalls, sometimes farther away, sometimes closer.

The ice was thin and brittle, so I moved to the right

on to a barely defined rib of rock and climbed up that instead. It was not very steep, but polished, sandy and streaming with water. Patches of fog kept forming and at times cloaked the whole face. Presently I found myself confronted with a particularly delicate series of moves. There was nowhere to place a piton, so I decided to take off the sack and leave it attached to the rope so that I could pull it up after me. On fingertips and tiptoes I had balanced up 5, 10, 15 metres, when suddenly I felt a kind of freezing sensation. It was as though the whole mountain were throbbing with the sound of a powerful aeroplane. For a moment I did not understand what was happening, then an incredible vision appeared through the cloud above me.

Against the white background a dark mass grew, exploded. It was as though the whole mountain were disintegrating and bursting out across the sky. There was no time to consider the matter: instinctively I flattened my body against the rock like a lizard. Blocks, boulders and splinters thudded and splattered against the slope or hooted past. I did not see them so much as perceive them with my entire being, their acrid odour penetrating down to my very lungs as I waited for the inevitable blow. Suddenly it came, powerful and burning. An intolerable pain spread through my chest, a horrible sensation as though my thorax was melting. For a moment I thought I had been knocked off into the air, but found myself still clinging to the rock with fingers that seemed to want to gouge into it. Now that it was past, it was difficult to tell whether it had lasted a few seconds or eternity. All that mattered was to be alive.

Around me the mountain was transformed, the ice black and pock-marked. Sand and splinters were still rolling and bouncing down, and indeed I was buried in them myself. My first cool thought was for the sack. Luckily it was still there in the hollow where I had left it; if it had been knocked off by the bombardment, it would certainly have dragged me down with it. I had to get out of my unnatural position and therefore climbed up a few metres, experiencing sharp pain in the back with every movement. Next I laboriously hauled up the sack. When it was still about 10 metres below me I noticed that the rope from which it was hanging was three-quarters cut through. Fortunately it stood up to the strain, and I was able to recover the precious sack. Meanwhile, I was growing more and more afraid. Heavy, weeping cloud-vapour had enveloped me, and above, unseen, more rocks were poised in balance, liable to fall on me at any moment. It was an uneasy cease-fire, giving a sensation of slow death. The rope was visibly cut in one place, but might well be so internally in others. Not all damage would necessarily show on the surface. In addition, one of my arms was hurting. Worst of all was my back, where the pain was really paralyzing—later, X-rays were to show that the left eleventh rib was fractured. I had a strong desire to get off the face, but by now the line of retreat was too exposed to stonefall. It therefore seemed best to move up to the right across the ice in the direction of a large rock that I had noted before the fog had formed, and which would offer me shelter for a bivouac. It took an age to reach, and when I got there I found that in reality it offered very little cover.

The north face of the Eiger (3,975 metres) from the flowery meadows of the Kleine Scheidegg.

Bonatti doing the Hinterstoisser traverse on the Eigerwand: 8 a.m. on 28 July 1963.

It began to rain, a thin, cold, irritating drizzle coming and going on a low wind like the breath of a sleeping dog. The whole mountain was soon streaming with water. My clothes were sopping right through to the last stitch, but I went on working in order to fashion myself a safe resting-place, hacking away ice, removing stones, placing pitons and fixing the rope until finally I could afford to take a rest. My bivouac thus began in the early afternoon.

Towards evening there was a shower of hail, after which the clouds began to break up, revealing increasingly large patches of blue sky. Through the straggling vapour shone a red disk more like the moon than the sun, now powerless to warm. The light was failing, and in the blue evening shadows white clouds sailed along the horizon. Almost certainly the next day would be fine, and indeed it was possible that down there in the valley today had been fine too. The Eiger often plays such tricks. Perhaps the sun had been shining brilliantly everywhere while the storm went round and round in the cauldron of the north face. The slow coming of night was hard to bear for the searing cold which penetrated my saturated garments and seemed to grasp me by the bone, while at every breath the pain in my left side was such that it felt as though my spine were being split in two.

Morning dawned radiantly fine. After the first pink and scarlet splendours, the snowy mountains on the horizon became honey-coloured, then reverted to white. The air was calm and cold; a few rounded, inoffensive clouds hung motionless here and there. I was exactly

H

half-way up the face, in the heart of the Eigerwand. By contrast with the remoteness of the north face of the Grandes Jorasses, that of the Eiger looks down on the centre of Grindelwald and its lush valley, so that the climber feels as though he were on the balcony of a high building. The contrast is striking, and in this too the Eiger is treacherous. It only needs a little cloud to surround you, and at once you feel cut off in an inferno of ice and death. The morning of which I speak, however, was so pervadingly peaceful that the features of the face seemed almost kindly and the snowfields innocuous. Reference points in the valley made me seem much higher than I really was, while the summit appeared invitingly close, attainable in no time at all. To obtain a more realistic estimate of the scale, however, one needed only to think of certain apparently insignificant fissures and ledges higher up, the names of which are chilling in their significance: the Ramp, the Traverse of the Gods, the White Spider.

There was something prodigious about it. Below me I could see people setting out over the green, spongy meadows, lined with sparkling brooks. Thin blue smoke rose from hamlets that still lay in shadow, slate roofs shone in the sun. Eastwards the dark pinewoods, still moist with dew, shimmered in the first misty rays. Each sound rose up to me with volume and clarity enhanced, vibrant in the air. I could hear the jangling and tinkling of grazing herds and, far off, the whistle of the little rack-railway train as it wound caterpillarwise in and out of the clumps of trees. It was somehow moving to think of it climbing, climbing all the way up to the Jungfraujoch at 3,457 metres, and also somewhat strange that on its way it would ascend in spirals through the bedrock of the mountain, under the very spot where I was sitting. The idea was absurd, like an incident in a dream.

I absorbed these sights during the moment of relaxation which follows even the most uncomfortable bivouac. Now it was time to think about my own situation, which since the day before had been sufficiently dramatic. My problem was to find the strength and control to get down without giving way to the paralyzing pain in my back. Presently, therefore, I slid out of the bivouac sack, knotted the ropes together and prepared the first of an interminable series of abseils. But there was a lump in my throat; I underwent a moment of indecision at the idea of giving up a long-cherished dream. Finally I made up my mind, or rather the mountain made it up for me. At first I had to clench my teeth for the pain, then gradually it became more bearable, affording me greater security. By comparison with the day before, the mountain seemed to be drowsing. Water, ice and stones were frozen into stillness. Certainly the warm weather had occasioned much of the stonefall, but the enormous landslide that had miraculously missed me by so little, merely spattering me in its passing, was undoubtedly an exceptional and unforeseeable event. In fifteen years of extreme mountaineering I had already survived similar occurrences on the north-west face of the Badile and the south-west pillar of the Dru, and was to do so again a year later on the Whymper spur of the Grandes Jorasses. I must admit my good luck, which always intervenes after an initial stroke of fate.

Once I had reversed the Hinterstoisser traverse I continued directly down in the plumbline from the Rote Fluh. At one point I saw some bleached bones in a deep, narrow crack. Undoubtedly they were human remains, witness of some unknown tragedy, but there was nothing I could do but pause for a moment in front of that natural tomb before continuing on my way.

So my dream of the Eiger came to an end. I had both lost and won, since at least I had returned alive where the other solo climbers had died. All in all, if not exactly satisfied, I was content. Moreover, the Eiger will always give relief rather than happiness; too often its ascent becomes a throw of the dice with life itself as the stake. It is an ugly mountain, squat, sombre, rotting away. And yet, as Harrer remarks, it is not so much a yardstick of the sheer ability of a climber as of his character and human quality. This is the true meaning of the ascent, as I had found out in my turn.

VII

The Coldest Place on Earth

IN ANTON TCHEKHOV's travel book *Siberia* there is a passage concerning the *taigà*, the virgin forest, which has always struck my imagination.

"Beyond the Yenisei," it runs, "begins the notorious *taigà* . . . the road runs continually between walls of birch, larch, spruce and pine . . . the spell of the *taigà* is neither in its trees nor its sepulchral silence, but in the fact that only the migrant birds know where it ends. For the first 24 hours you remain indifferent; for the second and third days you marvel at it; but only on the fifth or sixth day are you overcome with a sense of bewilderment and begin to wonder if you will ever succeed in escaping from this wonder of the world. You therefore climb to the top of some low wooded hill, look eastwards along the road, and see woods, then a low hill like a tangled curly head, then another beyond, and so on into infinity. After another 24 hours you climb another low hill, and there in front of you is the same panorama . . . nobody knows how many hundred versts the forest stretches, not even the stage-coach drivers and the peasants who were born there. Their imagination is livelier than ours, but they do not venture to set bounds to the *taigà*. In answer to our question they replied: 'It's endless.' They only know that in winter mysterious folk on reindeer come down out of the far north into the *taigà* to seek bread, but not even the oldest know who they are or where they come from."

I thought of that country as of a legend, supposing it impossible to visit on account of governmental restrictions and also fearing that those enchanted distances existed only in the poetic imagination of the great story-teller. But one day an opportunity arose to visit those outer limits of Siberia and measure their vastness with my own eyes, to touch the reality with my own hands.

For many years I had been sending articles on my adventures to the Italian weekly *Epoca*, and now the editor invited me to join a team of special reporters visiting the legendary "pole of cold". There were to be three of us: the journalist Brunello Vandano, the photographer Mario De Biasi and myself. At Moscow we were joined by the journalist Igor Antonov and the photographer Valeri Schustov, both of them Russian. We left the Soviet capital on 13 January 1964, with three weeks in which to reach and stay in the two coldest towns in the world, Verkhoiansk and Oymyakòn, where minimum temperatures of respectively $-69°C$ and $-71°C$ had been recorded.

I received my first impressions of the severe, boundless Siberia of the pioneers at Irkutsk, near the borders of Mongolia. On the banks of the Angara stood a monument to an eighteenth-century Russian expedition along this broad tributary of the Yenisei. The cold, though in no way unusual ($-25°C$), had frozen the surface to marble, and the river shipping, half drawn out of the water with the coming of winter, now stood up out of the opaque ice almost without contrast, like fossils in limestone.

At Yakutsk, some 2,000 kilometres farther north-east, the full severity of the Siberian winter was already in evidence. With its low, rough-hewn wooden houses, criss-crossed with electric wires and crusted with rime, its snow-encumbered streets and the grey mist wreathing around everything, Yakutsk is exactly how one would imagine the capital of an immense kingdom of frost, ten times as big as Italy but with a population of only half a million. Although the city is like an oasis of humanity in the midst of immeasurable emptiness, the atmosphere is still homely, with hotels, shops, factories, public transport and a big airport. Founded by the Cossacks in 1632, until recently it remained connected to the outer world only via the Lena, which flows into the Arctic Ocean. Nowadays it has become a city of 76,000 inhabitants, most of them indigenous, who mainly work in the gold-mining and pedigree fur industries.

It was the season of the *Kresccenie morosi*, the baptism of frost, and the thermometer stood at −50°C. We were, however, informed that at Verkhoiansk, where we were heading, it had gone down to −65°C. At temperatures like this it is impossible to get an aeroplane, as they do not risk taking off when the thermometer sinks below −57°C. There was thus nothing for it but to wait.

The days we spent in and around Yakutsk helped me to a better understanding of the people and landscape of the "pole of cold", and also to adapt myself physically so that I was better able to withstand the insidious cold during a long stay in the open in the *taigà*.

Our one-piece down-filled suits, the same as those used at 8,000 metres in the Himalayas, were the best that could be found on the market, and represented a rational substitute for the heavy fur clothing worn by the locals. By contrast, however, no western footwear formed any improvement over the *vaglienki*, the Russian felt boots. Keeping our hands warm proved no problem, since these are the easiest of all our members to regulate, and we simply wore more or fewer gloves as occasion demanded. As for our heads, we donned huge, soft, furry *ciapkas* over our balaclavas.

The intense cold showed no signs of abating. Nevertheless, our friends from the *Yauktsk Sovietskaia Gazieta* continued to put such pressure on the aircrew responsible that the pilots finally took their courage in both hands and decided to go. A man had been cut off by the ice for three months at a base on an island in the Arctic Ocean, and we provided a good pretext for going to his rescue. The aeroplane could drop us off at Verkhoiansk and pick us up on the way back without stopping its engines for fear they would not start again.

The preparations for take-off were long and laborious, but at last the twin-motored aircraft got away and set a course for the mysterious north. For about half an hour the Lena wound below us, and despite its 15 kilometre width it seemed no more than a barely perceptible white ribbon amid the all-prevailing whiteness around. Finally it curved away to the left and was lost on the hazy horizon. Ahead, the profile of the Verkhoiansk range, which we had to cross, began to take shape. The foothills were thickly wooded, then the mountains rose higher and became bare, gradually folding into ridges and peaks from which the radiant light cast long shadows. Throughout virtually the whole trip the temperature on board the aircraft was −20°C.

We landed on a vast pearly plain, raising a cloud of frost particles. There were no signs of any village, but on a small tower of red-varnished wood towards which we taxied stood a notice in Cyrillic lettering which presumably said "Verkhoiansk Airport". Over the building rose a single, slender aerial, the pole of cold's connection with the rest of the world.

Traditionally, Verkhoiansk is considered as the pole of cold, although strictly speaking the lowest temperature (−71°C) was recorded at Oymyakòn, 500 kilometres farther south-east. Apart from the latitude—Verkhoiansk is well within the Arctic Circle—the factors accounting for the climate are the Verkhoiansk and Tcherski ranges, 2,000–3,000 metres high, which shelter this already continental region from the winds, notably the warmer air currents from the Arctic Ocean. Although the latter is farther north, the fact that it is liquid makes it a good heat conductor relative to the dry land. Here behind the ranges, as on a dead planet, the frost settles and stagnates throughout the sunless winter. For the same reasons, in summer, when the sun never sets, the heat becomes almost intolerable. Another consequence of the terrain is that it virtually never rains or snows, though in winter the landscape lies blanched under a soft pall of powdery frost crystallized out of the small content of humidity in the air, which often forms dense fog.

As we climbed down from the plane, smoking as though on fire, the −20°C inside it seemed like +20°C by comparison with the temperature outside. A man popped up from nowhere, dark and spherical in his brown-bear overcoat. He signed to us to follow. He spoke no Russian, and in his efforts to make himself understood he ended by undoing the long *papirosa* he had been holding tightly between his teeth. It seemed that he was trying to explain that the thermometer was hovering around −70°C. His disappointment was visible when he discovered that we were not Chinese. In the meantime a tracked vehicle had driven up. From it, clad in a coat of red fox fur, descended the president of the local Soviet, who had been notified of our arrival by radio from Yakutsk and had hastened to greet us. He drove us to the village ten minutes away by road. The man was a typical Yakut, short and stumpy, slit-eyed, flat-featured, wrinkled, with a permanent half-smile and an enigmatic expression. He was kindly, and apparently spoke fluent Russian, but was extremely sparing of words with our Muscovite colleagues, who in these surroundings felt just as foreign as us. The language we spoke with Antonov and Schustov was French, but to communicate with the locals we often required two interpreters, one translating from French into Russian, the other from Russian into Yakut and back again.

Once we reached the village, which resembled Yakutsk except that it was smaller and the houses poorer, De Biasi and I left the others. My friend was attracted principally by people and their homes; I wandered off into the *taigà* towards the broad, frozen Yana river, which I had already glimpsed from the aeroplane. Rivers hold a particular fascination for me, perhaps on account of that atavism which has always suggested them to men as the natural roadways of the Earth.

After a couple of hours, the cold which had struck us like a fist in the face as we left the aeroplane began to penetrate our clothes, cancelling their thermal properties and striking through to the skin. Our bodies were swiftly numbed. In other circumstances I might have reacted by running or doing physical jerks in order to generate warmth in my muscles, but here such action would have been dangerous. The effort would have made me pant, causing the air to reach the lungs at too low a temperature and thus injuring them. It was essential to find a pace that would enable us to move and endure without endangering our safety. This is one of the secrets of survival at the pole of cold.

The white, soft, yet hard-frozen *taigà* through which I was making my way was powerful and sinister. Coated in rime, the tree-trunks towered bonily against the sky, their immobile branches like coral, a forest of giant acropora on the bed of a dried-out sea. After no more than a few hundred metres one has the feeling of being trapped in a mortally dangerous labyrinth. Woe to anyone who has no sense of direction and allows himself to become a prey to panic! But at the same time the *taigà* is marvellous and inspiring. What could be more beautiful, more moving than this wild, mysterious aspect of nature where man must open his own trail? Every step forward is a problem and an act of will. Direction assumes a significance, almost a colour, and the very air seems to acquire scent and consistency. The sensitivity that nature calls out of a man is prodigious, but nevertheless it is strange how one may love and fear a thing simultaneously. Perhaps the mystery of humanity resides precisely in this atavistic contradiction.

The forest consists mainly of conifers, neither particularly high nor thick in the trunk, but dense and tangled. A good half of them are broken with age or frost, which splits the trunks if they have absorbed too much water during the summer. It is astonishing how the plant-life has adapted itself to the rigours of the Siberian winter. In these regions the land never thaws out beyond a depth of a metre or two, below which subsists the 600 metre-deep *merzlotà*, or ground which has remained in a permafrost since remote ages. It is in this layer that the remains of mammoths are sometimes found perfectly preserved in the iron-hard subsoil. On encountering this sterile surface the roots of trees spread out horizontally for many metres, compensating for their lack of depth with the breadth of their base.

I reached the Yana. Like the Lena it seemed made of alabaster, veined and wrinkled by the impact of ice-floes borne along on the current at the beginning of winter when the crust is still fragile. They say that the ice is a metre and a half deep at this point. Wandering upstream, I heard a sound of bells somewhere beyond a wide curve. Presently a sleigh emerged from the *taigà* drawn by two white horses, shaggy as polar bears. Two men enveloped in dark furs climbed down from the sleigh and led the horses out into the middle of the river where there was a collection of bluish mounds, around which they began to busy themselves. Now I understood: they had come to collect blocks of ice to take home and melt for water. As I drew nearer we exchanged simple greetings as though we had known each other all our lives. Then, strangely indifferent to my presence, my race, my different physical characteristics and my unusual clothing, they quietly went on with their work. I walked on towards Verkhoiansk along the trail from which the sleigh had appeared. Darkness thickened among the trees; the sun glimmered low and dull through the fiery clouds on the horizon. It was in fact just 2 o'clock in the afternoon, but I might have been looking at a dawn or sunset at home. Far ahead of me the blue smoke from the chimneys rose against the sky like the beginning of a forest fire.

Two days later we went on to Oymyakòn, literally the coldest place on Earth. As in practically all the villages in outer Siberia, the people here live from fishing, hunting for furs, and above all from rearing reindeer. Whereas the fishing is interrupted when the rivers freeze over, the other activities incredibly continue throughout the year, keeping men and beasts utterly isolated in the *taigà*. In order to learn something of the hardships of their lives we spent a few days with these Yakuts in their village cabins and in the tents of hunters and herdsmen out in the forest. We travelled about sometimes on foot, sometimes in sleighs drawn by reindeer, and sometimes riding on their backs like the herdsmen themselves.

Indoors, the houses are kept extraordinarily hot. They nearly all have three series of doors with spaces between them in order to conserve the heat better. A massive structure of pale stalactites encrusts the porches of the houses and hangs outside every window. These are the product of the sum of tiny air leaks which instantly crystallize as they encounter the outer cold. Inside their *iurte* or cabins, the Yakuts live almost naked. Before going outside they dress up heavily, and the accumulated heat is such that thus bundled up they can stay warm for at least a couple of hours, longer than which they never expose themselves to the cold when living a village life.

In the *laigà* the men live a nomadic existence, taking turns for a fortnight or a month with the hunting or herding. Throughout this time a fire burns constantly in each man's tent. However, in order to carry out chores and skin animals they are obliged to leave the tents open, and they therefore ingeniously keep three or four fires burning around the camp—there is never any shortage of wood—thus creating an insulating ring of air which, if not exactly balmy, is at least at a bearable temperature.

In this region they hunt sable, ermine, squirrel, red and blue fox, wolf and, before they hibernate, brown bear. Sometimes the herdsmen are hunters too, and both live mainly off their prey and off their reindeer. When they get back to their warm villages they still eat reindeer, but otherwise mainly elk and wild horse. These meats they cook in various ways or make into *pépelni*, a kind of ravioli, adding a spice of variety with fish out of the river eaten cold and raw, cut into filleted strips called *straganina*. Such dishes are seasoned with reindeer-milk products such as *suaghèi*, a thick cold cream, or *tchokòn*, small frozen lumps of milk emulsion.

The Yakuts only eat once a day, but the meal is a

veritable banquet. Usually it begins with cold dishes, followed by warm ones and finishing with boiling tea. They say that this age-old system is good for the digestion and for the teeth. I never succeeded in finding out exactly what was a matter of course and what was due to hospitality, but whichever it was, this massive test of bodily capacity was immediately followed by the opening of bottles of spirits which were imbibed in the cause of Yakuti-Italian friendship. There was therefore no escaping from these libations, which followed each other with terrifying frequency. Vermouth, the least alcoholic drink, being reserved exclusively for women, even the soberest of men has to start straight in with vodka. But the real drink of your genuine Siberian is pure alcohol. In Moscow, when Doctor Nikolai Danilov, Director of the Novòsti, had told us about this with a broad smile, I had not believed him. The dire fact is that they pour out half glasses of the stuff, which you are obliged to swallow in one gulp if you do not wish to provoke any doubts as to your virility. It is customary to follow this with a swig of water, but without breathing in between. Meanwhile everyone talks, jokes and sings.

Even when there is no drink around, the songs of the Yakuts are moving and beautiful. They are of obviously Cossack origin. The women have the softness and skill of orientals, while the men possess a vivacity unknown among other Arctic peoples. The children burst out of school in a joyous frenzy, bouncing and scampering like squirrels in the spring. The people are healthy and long-lived; the eighty-five-year-old Dmitri Gromov, for ex-ample, never misses a chance to go hunting in the *taigà*. Roman Ivanovich Brisgailov, a member of the Supreme Soviet of the Autonomous Republic of Yakutia and head of the 100 *sovkos* scattered around the territory, is everyone's friend and available at all times and places to help solve a problem or attend a ceremony. During our visit, however, nobody else could get through to him, as he was busy looking after his strange guests from far away.

At the pole of cold you feel nature to be utterly indifferent to the sufferings of man. For nine months of the year the people virtually never take off their gloves and stretch their fingers. They certainly did not come here from choice or to find a promised land, yet they have adapted themselves amazingly well to the conditions and on the whole things are not too bad. The only creatures that still suffer are the reindeer, incessantly exposed to all the rigours of the climate. You see them in the *taigà* wandering through the snow, scraping here and there with their hooves to get at the sparse lichen on which they feed. When they find it they bury their muzzles dramatically in the white frost powder that burns like fire. And so it goes on throughout the long, pitiless winter, unless one day they sink to the ground out of weakness, there to remain glued by their own swiftly frozen urine.

Among the hills surrounding the wide plain of Oymyakòn there was one, higher than the rest, that remained shining when the others were long sunk in night. What would the view be like from up there? One day I took the decision to tell my friends of my desire to climb it. At first Roman Ivanovich was very reluctant

Reindeer grazing at around noon in the *taigà* near Oymyakòn, the coldest place on earth.

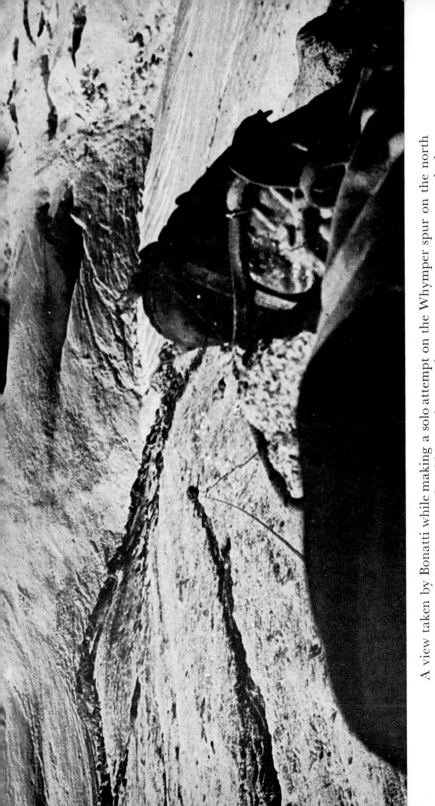

A view taken by Bonatti while making a solo attempt on the Whymper spur on the north face of the Grandes Jorasses. On this occasion a point over 3,500 metres was reached.

to let me go; then, perhaps remembering how often he had caught me gazing towards it, he resigned himself to one more responsibility rather than disappoint me.

The first rays of the brief day surprised me puffing my way up the steep hillside, which was unexpectedly tiring. I was on my own, wading through a carpet of snow nearly half a metre deep and so ridiculously soft, dry and floury that it offered no resistance whatever to my light *vaglienki*. My feet sank through as though someone were shifting it aside so that I could place my feet directly on the hard, slippery hillside beneath. The soft felt could get no grip on this surface and I skidded abominably, panting with the effort of remaining upright. The air I breathed carefully in through my nose issued more rapidly through my half-closed lips with a kind of whistling sound, thick with vapour, like a steam loco-motive standing in a station after a long journey. The phenomenon, normal enough in these parts, was due to the speed with which the breath condenses when the temperature descends below —50°C. The locals had already told me about it as an empirical method of judging extreme temperatures.

Every so often the air began to smell of ammonia and taste of ether, and then I would have to stop and get my breath. The thermometer I had had made specially for this trip showed that it was —60°C.

At last I found myself on the broad summit of the hill, dazzled with reflected light. New horizons rose stiff and enchanted before me. The curiously snow-encrusted spruce-trees recalled images from childhood tales that began with "Once upon a time . . ." The coldly blazing sunlight sparkled off the thousands of tiny crystals stirred up by my passing. The only other thing that moved was my shadow, elongated and silent as all it touched. There were no tracks: neither bear nor famished wolf would dream of climbing up here.

I took photographs until the three cameras I carried froze up one after the other despite being kept under my parka when not in use, but not before they had cut up the films they contained, rendered brittle by the frost. Fortunately the air is extremely dry, or one would never survive. A few days earlier, my breath had been sufficient to freeze the view-finder of the camera to my right eyebrow, causing an irritating open wound.

The magical hour of sunset arrived; a sunset utterly, almost unreasonably still. The bright curve of the summit was outlined against the flatlands, fast fading into the grey shadow that foreran the night. The disk of the sun sank behind the dark waves of the hills, tinting the sky briefly yellow. Over my shoulder, above the spruces that seemed to be driving their pointed tops right into the sky, a huge three-quarter moon was already shining. The north was an empty space verging on nothing, but against the mauve sky past Oymyakòn were silhouetted shapes full of mystery, the Tcherski mountains, a range as long as the Alps and only "discovered" in 1926. There is the source of the great Indigirka river that runs across these plains. Near its springs lies the fabled lake of Lambankur which mysteriously never quite freezes over and in whose depths lives a dreadful monster, perhaps an ichthyosaurus, which sometimes emerges snorting. No Yakut would dream of visiting this sinister spot.

Infinitely remote and far away, a few tiny lights began to twinkle across the level forest to the profound silence of this look-out at the limit of the world, where the feeling of space grows acute and the void seems to spread ever wider. It was Oymyakòn. The white ground at my feet was now black. In the abyss of the sky points of light came to life, flickering and faintly pulsing. The universe was giving back the movement stilled by the great cold.

VIII

The Whymper Spur

THE DATE WAS 7 July 1964. For the fifth time in two summers I was tramping up the Leschaux glacier with the object of attempting the unclimbed north spur of the Pointe Whymper on the Grandes Jorasses. Each time I had been foiled by bad weather, dangerous thaw or a falling barometer before even reaching the foot of the face, except on one occasion the previous year when I had been accorded the pleasure of crossing the bergschrund only to have to turn back immediately.

Seen from directly in front, the great trapezoidal north face of the Grandes Jorasses diminishes in size at its left end and even more so on the right, where it almost merges into the glacier descending from the col of the same name. But the real north face in the climbing sense consists of the regular, architecturally harmonious series of ribs and gullies descending from the Pointes Walker, Whymper and Croz, which endow it with its sublime austerity. By contrast with the two parallel ribs on either side of it, the Whymper spur falls direct from the summit to merge into a steep, sombre, icy re-entrant in the face, and its angle, difficulty and objective danger are correspondingly greater. It is hardly ever touched by the sun.

The spell this route cast over me stemmed from the

fact that it had all the qualities that lend fascination to a route. The difficulties and dangers were very great, yet of a traditional kind, proper to the character and atmosphere of the north face in general. And indeed the spur stood for the alpha and omega of its gripping story. In 1931, when the whole wide face still remained to be explored, it was this very re-entrant which appealed logically to the expert Brehm and Rittler, who chose to attack at this point. How they met their deaths is not known; their friends found the shattered bodies at the foot of the slope while going up to attempt the face in their turn. From that time on nobody had dared to attempt the route again.

So for the fifth time I stood below the bergschrund. It was still night. Around me all was silent save for the dripping of the ice stalactites hanging from the upper rim of the schrund, a sound that reverberated in the motionless air. In this hour before the dawn, however, everything should have been immobilized by the frost. The sky was clear, the mountain peaceful, but in some strange way it did not feel right. I could not make up my mind to attack. Dawn came, and shortly afterwards, for no reason that I could explain, I turned back. As I walked back up the Mer de Glace I noted a great coming and going of helicopters around the Aiguille Verte. Later I learned that at the very time when I had been standing hesitant and uncertain at the bergschrund a terrible Alpine disaster had taken place, perhaps the worst ever caused by thaw. In the Cordier couloir of the Aiguille Verte the unexpected collapse of a cornice had carried down fourteen guides and candidate guides of the École Nationale de Ski et d'Alpinisme, among them the former world skiing champion Charles Bozon.

On 24 July I returned to the Whymper spur, this time alone, in accordance with an impulse of desire for and resentment against this "inviolable" wall. This time it yielded to my insistence, allowing me to make my way up its treacherous armour of steep, brittle ice, though truly I was like the prey in the jaws of a monster. On this grandiose, severe face, I rediscovered the exaltation of a lonely struggle with the mountain, in which all emotions are magnified and sensitivity and reactions sharpened. I remember that one journalist, who credited me with "the fanaticism of the prophets and the obstinacy of a maniac", defined my mountaineering philosophy as "a stupidly sterile, self-sufficing audacity". For my part, however, I consider that if everybody were given the chance of undergoing similar experiences they would acquire a much better comprehension of themselves and others. They might also understand that humanity has changed and no longer knows how to live. As though it were gone crazy, it constantly imprisons itself in its own myths and ambitions, rushing from one servitude to another. Is it not perhaps true that, in liberating itself from certain forms of oppression, mankind is falling into the opposite tyranny of a collectivism which systematically objectifies people, reducing them to statistics? Man seems to be positively at pains to dehumanize himself, to abandon all that is most positive in his nature. In his egoism, he does not even hesitate to upset the balance of nature, extending the harm to other living creatures. Every source of life is contaminated. Nowadays a high proportion of illness is caused not by bacteria and other micro-organisms but by chemical agents. Anyone who considers the problem objectively and scientifically in the hope of forecasting the future cannot fail to be depressed.

Meanwhile, we continue to ignore and aggravate the problem, hastening our own decline. The statistics speak for themselves: within a few decades the population of the world will be doubled, and what then? Shall we find an outlet in other planets, or having reduced ourselves to the only expression of life in an otherwise sterile universe, shall we die slowly of our own toxic waste-products? Perhaps only the fittest will survive—but will there still be any fittest?

We are in fact regressing. Alienation, inability to communicate, anxiety, indifference, moral apathy: these are realities which give the measure of modern man, born of a society that seems to think only in terms of power and the good life. Practically nobody is interested any more in the authentic values.

So what have we become? Not animals certainly, but not truly human either, a sort of hybrid monster tyrannizing over ourselves and others, polluted down to the very springs of our vital instincts. What has brought us so low? Is it technology seducing us with facile well-being only to degenerate us with each success, destroying one by one our ideals and myths, replacing them with calculation, dismaying emptiness, the terror of what the future may bring? Is our all-powerful science to blame, increasingly excluding us from the oligarchy of its followers? It would be easy to believe this if one were not aware that philosophy, religion and society in general are only too ready to palm off the responsibility for all our ills on it. The fact of the matter is that, weighed down with his inherited burden of weaknesses, man has lagged behind his own level of awareness. A glance at our present society is almost enough to make one long for a more primitive state of being; yet our way lies forward and not back. Even if, for the sake of argument, we were able to demolish our existing social structures and revert to our original condition, how would we survive, denatured as we are and multiplied like locusts? Such an inquisition may be profoundly disturbing, but it is absolutely useless to cry over our fate. As products of an ineluctable cosmic phenomenon, we must just resign ourselves to being children of our time. But if this is the case, why do we not live our own time properly? What does it help us to possess all that progress has placed at our service when we have lost all sense of the meaning of things and even of life itself? Unfortunately, peace does not come naturally to man, and rarely suits his disposition. On the contrary, aggressiveness has always been congenial to him, and it is true that without it we would never have shown any signs of personality or respect. Nevertheless, there it is: we have this re-grettable legacy of every source of life and violence. Aggression is of our very nature, and today more than ever expresses itself in rebellion and demonstration against inherited structures, now thought unacceptable.

We have always had something with which to re-proach preceding generations; yet if it were not so we would perhaps have remained reptiles or mere hominoids. In our modern revolt there is often a passive aggression, sometimes not without an aspect of violence. The passivity of modern man, the way in which he gets swept up in any protest movement, seem to me an absolute refusal of awareness and of any objective analysis of the very motives of his revolt. Many fail to understand this. It cannot be explained to them, since the tale is the history of mankind itself, made up of contradictions, of "useful" and "useless" things, of conflicting and often irreconcilable visions of life.

In intimate relation with nature I gradually made my way up into the heart of the mountain wall. Everything here induced reflection, reducing the most deep-rooted illusions of strength and endurance to a realization of fragility. There were 500 metres of shining ice beneath my feet. Above, by contrast, the remaining 600 metres of wall seemed ready to fall over me, a vista of snow-plastered bulges dense as the foam on a glass of new-drawn beer. In such conditions there could be no question of continuing.

In a melancholy mood I climbed back down until the setting sun forced me to search for a bivouac ledge. Only in the chill of dawn would it be possible to descend the final ice-gully in safety.

To break the spell of my successive failures on the Whymper spur, I climbed the hitherto virgin north buttress of the Trident de Tacul on 30 July. This gave a fine, exposed route up compact, vertical granite, and difficult into the bargain. Already a ski champion, my companion, the Alpini Sergeant Livio Stuffer, proved himself a fine rock-climber. I thus regained my good humour, which the series of debacles on the Whymper had been fraying.

Back at home, however, a depressing surprise was waiting for me. It was 31 July 1964, the anniversary of the ascent of K 2, the second highest mountain in the world (8,611 m). Ten years earlier I had had the honour of taking part in the victorious Italian expedition. Now a newspaper made use of the occasion to create a sensation at my expense by publishing an article in which it appeared that my conduct during the expedition had been treacherous, lying, incompetent and generally vile. What worse could be said of a man?

Naturally, I know the rules of the game where "personalities" are concerned—the reader will excuse me if this sounds conceited—but this time they were digging into a painful old wound which had not healed easily. I am increasingly convinced that tolerance is a legacy from an earlier age and can no longer be pre-supposed a virtue in the world in which we live. Often it solves nothing, but even aggravates, causing imputations and consquences to fall on our own heads. On this occasion I therefore felt that I could not suffer such slander in silence; those who had struck this dirty blow should serve as an example. The riposte should be rational and adapted to our time. I therefore brought an action for libel against the newspaper in question. Two years later my reputation was publicly restored when, after considering all the evidence, the court recognized that the truth of the matter was as set out in my book *Le mie montagne*.* Yet to have this affair thrown up at me after

* See footnote, p. 57.

ten years, disturbing my feelings and my existence, was like a bitter regurgitation. However, I did not brood over it, but returned with all the more passion to the conquest of the Whymper spur, which for me had become a symbolic challenge.

For the seventh time I climbed up to the foot of the face, only to be turned back by bad weather. Well, too bad. Soon there would be an eighth. When I got home I found the Genevan climber Michel Vaucher waiting for me. I had not seen him for a year, and in the warmth of our meeting I mentioned the project which had now become an obsession with me, telling him about my hopes and vicissitudes. Finally, seeing a spark of enthusiasm in his eye, I blurted out: "What about joining me for the next attempt?" Naturally he agreed, and his obvious pleasure made me supremely happy in turn.

At 3 o'clock in the morning of Thursday, 6 August, our head-torches shone on the frightening ice-slopes with which the climb begins. The mountain was frozen into stillness, though by daylight this zone is an inferno of falling boulders. Without delay, I began nicking steps in the bare ice. The cold was not too excessive—just a few degrees below zero, enough to hold the stones in their place. As we climbed, the weight of our sacks began to make itself felt. We had with us everything needed for a major enterprise: two 40 metre ropes, fifty pitons, thirty karabiners, four étriers, two hammers, bivouac sacks, a cooker and supplies for five days. Our crampons were on our feet, our axes in our hands, and we would obtain water by melting ice and snow.

By dawn we were already at 3,100 metres. Up to this

point we had moved without exchanging a word, climbing automatically, each sunk in his own thoughts. I would chop my way up each rope-length, then my companion would join me. Now that it was daylight I continued to hack away, presently noting a star still shining over the Pointe Whymper. It was Venus. It reminded me of how many years previously I had seen a similarly bright star when climbing the Cerro Adela in Patagonia. That time it had been a good omen. As I climbed on, my thoughts ran back until I hardly noticed my present situation. The spell was broken by a shower of stones, which gave us occasion to exchange views for the first time. Apart from the stonefall, we agreed that on this lower part of the wall conditions could hardly be better. It was the first time we had been together on a major climb, but our teamwork was perfect right from the start and somehow I felt the conviction that, after my seven setbacks, this time everything was set for success. In this kind of undertaking patience and perseverance are almost always rewarded in the end.

Presently we reached the first rocks. These proved to be almost free of snow, and, as the ice couloir now lay below us, we took off our crampons, leading alternate pitches. Progress was rapid and exciting. I am not used to being led on climbs and thus rarely quite trust the man above me, no matter how expert he may be, but with Vaucher it was different. Together with Pierre Mazeaud and Carlo Mauri, who have been my comrades in many an adventure in the Alps and farther afield, he is the only person with whom I feel quite safe when his turn comes to lead—as safe as if I were leading myself.

As during the preceding few days the weather was splendid, and there were so many parties on the face that it had lost something of its usual austerity. I gazed across at the Walker spur, only a few hundred metres away and parallel with the buttress on which we stood. It would always be a superb climb with a great name, but I reflected with some bitterness that it could scarcely be called an exploit any more. In fact it was literally swarming with ropes; no greater contrast could have been imagined with the absolute loneliness of our first winter ascent in 1963 or the imposing reputation which the route still enjoyed when I had climbed it in August 1949. Now there was a continuous line of figures from base to summit like an interminable trail of ants on the trunk of a tree. The chatter and shouting in a variety of languages sounded like an oriental bazaar. The only noise missing was that of hammer on piton; obviously the route must be bristling with them. From our standpoint it was as though all these crowds were thronging another world.

At 10 o'clock I reached the point where I had bivouacked two weeks earlier, a small ledge about 1 metre by 80 centimetres on which we found a packet of sugar and two of biscuits still in good condition. It seemed a good spot to take a short rest. Twenty metres below, Vaucher was getting ready to join me. I called out to him to traverse out to the left and fill his canteen from a copious runnel. Hardly had I taken in the rope to belay him when without any warning two huge boulders came whirring down and burst into fragments on the rock above us. I just had time to yell "Michel!" and flatten myself against the wall. The blast moved my right foot as a rock zoomed past, missing it by two centimetres and Vaucher by not much more. As it struck the ledge it cut the loosely coiled rope into five pieces. I picked them up; they were still hot from the impact. It made me tremble to think of my last bivouac, or to imagine what could have become of my foot. However, the most urgent problem was what to do about the rope. The incident was more serious than it might seem. We had climbed barely a quarter of the face, and both our ropes were sliced into bits, the longest of which measured about 22 metres. Should we turn back? We hardly even considered the idea, though aware that we were going to have complications, since in order to proceed we should have to tie the longest lengths together, which would call for some strange manœuvres on account of the fact that the knots would not slide through any karabiners.

Before continuing we munched some lumps of sugar and swigged the water which Vaucher had scooped up from the runnel. As we set off again the sun, which had been slanting down on us for about an hour, disappeared behind the summit ridge for the rest of the day. At once the air turned colder and the face assumed a grimmer aspect.

We continued patiently making our way up pitches which I already knew from my solo attempt. The slabby rock was extremely steep, and we had a few more dangerous stonefalls to dodge. Late in the afternoon we reached my previous highest point. Shortly afterwards Vaucher called down from above: "Walter, did you get as far as this?"

"No," I replied, "only as far as where I'm standing now."

"Well, there's a piton here."

And so there was. Old, rusty and well driven home, it undoubtedly dated from the time of the first attempts on the face. It was a real collector's item, but when Vaucher tried to get it out it resisted his efforts sturdily. We therefore decided to leave it in place as a memorial to those who had fallen, perhaps from this very point, namely the German climbers Rittler and Brehm, whose bodies were found at the foot of the central ice-couloir in August 1931.

The rest of the afternoon passed uneventfully. Evening found us preparing to bivouac on a couple of flakes of rock in the shelter of an enormous bulge, under which we fixed two lengths of rope to speed up our departure the following morning. The weather seemed set fair. As increasing cold put a stop to the rockfalls and darkness stilled the noisy procession on the Walker spur, silence settled again over the mountain. Vaucher and I were perched each on his own flake, about 15 metres apart. Neither of us spoke. Gradually we drifted off to sleep in the total darkness that engulfed us.

I woke with a jump: the rock was shuddering as though in an earthquake. I had a terrifying sensation of falling . . . no, it was the mountain collapsing around us. As I stared up through the blackness I saw the slope beginning to give off fire as though a volcanic eruption were taking place. The air was full of a deafening, terrifying, continuous roar. In a moment the fire was pouring towards us, was upon us, incredibly passing over us. By its light I saw dark blocks the size of railway carriages thudding into the face. Each blow struck another fountain of sparks, while all around everything was pulverized and disintegrated. I heard myself yelling as I flattened myself against the rock, trying to retract my head into my shoulders, to disappear completely; then I stopped thinking at all and simply waited. A blast of air squeezed me against the wall, taking my breath away.

The rumbling became less intense, the showers of boulders and sparks continued on their way towards the glacier. I was completely buried in stone and ice rubble, a freezing shower which was almost pleasant as being a sign that I was still alive. But what had become of Vaucher? Before the thought was complete I was calling out his name, just as his voice rose up from below calling mine. The mountainside was now still again as though nothing had happened, but I was seized with uncontrollable fits of trembling that only gradually faded out into sleep.

As daylight came the mountainside revealed itself transformed, almost planed. Projections and ledges had been shoved off by the thousands of tons of falling rock that we could now see spread out below us on the glacier that was blackened and ironed flat for hundreds of metres. The first three huge crevasses and séracs had entirely disappeared.

Leaning back, I succeeded in picking out the place from which the landslip had fallen. An enormous pinnacle some 120 metres high was missing and in its place was a broad apse-shaped recess of pale rock, seamed

Vaucher seconding a pitch on the third day of the first ascent of the Whymper spur (8 August 1964).

Three Bonatti routes:
- - - - - - the east face of the Grand Capucin, 20–23 July 1961
———— the west face of the Trident (18 September 1963)
. . . . . . the north face of the Trident (30 July 1964).

with ice. Obviously the pinnacle's collapse had been caused by a slow, natural process that had been going on for who knows how many years. However that might be, we now had to climb up the path it had followed. Holds and cracks had been razed out of existence, but the most worrying thing was the great slabs that remained teetering on the edge of the scar. As the temperature rose they were bound to start falling, and we were right in the line of fire. We therefore resolved to take full advantage of the morning chill to climb as far as possible before the sunlight should touch the face.

The ropes fixed the evening before helped us off to a quick start, but the thaw was almost as prompt in arriving. We had only reached the second rope when the first stonefalls whizzed by only a few metres away. I raised my head to look up, and suddenly it was as though I had been struck by lightning; a stone hit me full in the face with such violence that I was almost knocked off. I was hanging on to the rope with my hands alone and no security whatever, and now I found myself blinded with copiously flowing blood. Paralyzed with pain, I remained where I was for fear of fainting and letting go. Ten metres below, Vaucher had seen what had happened, but was in no position to help. With an effort I succeeded in controlling myself and hauled up on my arms until I reached the peg to which the rope was fixed. Here I clung on while feeling the wound: it was deep and sticky. Now my nose began to bleed as well. I broke off an icicle and pressed it to my forehead, the top of my head, and the base of my nose, but all to no avail. I mopped away uselessly with my handkerchief. Slowly the

K

pain became more bearable, but I was obsessed with the idea of not being able to stop the bleeding and therefore climbed back down to Vaucher and then on to the bivouac ledge. My friend looked after me as best he could, binding up the wound with a dressing. Finally I sat astride a protected flake, leant back my head as far as possible and remained quite still. At first the blood blocked up my throat, but finally the flow ceased.

The bombardment had now become so intense that for an hour and a half we remained where we were. At last the sun passed behind the crest of the mountain, the temperature fell and the stonefalls became less frequent. It was 9.30 when we started off for the second time, moving fast so as to gain ground before the monster should awake again. Progress was awkward and nerve-racking, since the holds had disappeared, leaving a kind of sandy paste frozen to the rock. At midday we attained a niche right under the scar where the pillar had fallen away. Here we had to halt, as the rockfalls had started again with renewed violence. The weather also showed signs of breaking, and towards 2 o'clock a hailstorm broke over us which lasted on and off until about 6, when the air got cold again.

As on the previous evening we fixed the two longest pieces of rope—one of 18 metres, the other of 22—up the first pitch we would have to climb next day, a kind of ice-groove under the left edge of the scar. We were now at a height of about 3,700 metres, and in a whole day had succeeded in making just 100 metres of progress. Neither of us considered the idea of retreat. For one thing the remaining pieces of rope were too short, and for another the danger in the area swept by the landslide, i.e. practically the whole way down, would be so great as to classify any attempt as madness.

Our second bivouac was even more uncomfortable than the first. I managed to catch in a plastic bag some water dripping from an overhang, so that after we had eaten a little we were able to quench our thirst. No sooner had we pulled on our bivouac sacks than a thunderstorm broke over us. The thunder and lightning went on for a long time accompanied by hail which later gave place to snow. It then snowed throughout the night.

At dawn on Saturday it was still snowing softly. A few hours later the sky cleared, revealing a mountain utterly transformed. Before us the Walker spur was cleansed of its crowds. There were just four little dark dots bunched together on what had now become a pale sheet of ice 1,200 metres high. Out of all those that had thronged the buttress during the previous few days these two parties had been caught by the bad weather at two-thirds height. As I looked at those four men I felt afraid for them; then I thought to myself that if they had seen us they would be even more afraid for us. Henceforward we had to find a way up whatever the cost, even if we could only gain 50 metres per day. There was no alternative.

As on the day before, the stonefall began soon after dawn. Towards 9 o'clock it seemed to be getting rarer, so we forced ourselves to start climbing again. The route lay up an icy drain, terribly steep and difficult, and the next few score metres held us up for two hours. We were about half-way up this stretch when another load of rocks came bombing down on us, thundering into the wall very close to Vaucher. He was unhurt, but one of our two remaining lengths of rope was cut through just 3 metres from his waist-loop.

We had now been living for two days under a rain of tumbling blocks, and this latest incident left us unmoved. We simply continued on the single rope up the edge of the scar. It had become so difficult to find any security that after running out 18 metres of rope we sometimes still had not discovered anywhere to place a piton. According to the rules, in such circumstances the second should remain anchored, but we were constrained to untie and start climbing in order to enable the leader to reach the next stance. In this way we continued leading through.

At last we escaped from the landslide zone, continuing for the rest of the day up ice- and snow-plastered chimneys and overhangs. Much of the climbing was at the limits of the possible. Sometimes we had to surmount compact, almost vertical walls of granite coated with ice only a few centimetres thick which might suddenly give way under our feet, and this without any belays whatsoever. It was almost evening when in the course of hammering in a piton I gave myself a tremendous blow on the thumb. For a moment the pain was so terrible that I almost fainted, then it abated somewhat and I was able to continue.

We installed our third bivouac in the depths of an icy recess which we called "the spider" by analogy with the similar feature on the Eiger. During the day we had climbed 250 metres; there remained about the same

Bonatti on the first ascent of the north-east spur of the Punta Innominata (3,732 metres).

An ice-fall on Mont Blanc.

Panei on the "Traverse of the Angels", north face of the Matterho

distance to the summit. The weather was improving, and this had a good effect on our morale in spite of the fact that the face was still plastered in snow. Before it became quite dark I followed my usual custom of fixing a rope up the next pitch so as to get a quick start next morning.

We were now close to 4,000 metres. After crawling around in the snow all day long we were soaked to the skin, and as darkness fell it became exceptionally cold for the time of year, perhaps because the favourable north wind was ousting the west. The thermometer presently sank to $-15°C$.

Nowhere on the whole face was there a bivouac site where two could settle down side by side. A rocky rib provided us with perches which we had to hack clear of ice. Though closer than during the two previous nights, we were still separated. Two metres below me, balancing a solid-fuel cooker, Vaucher was brewing a hot drink; only now did we realize that we had eaten and drunk practically nothing all day. I was still busy looking for ways of improving our anchorage. Suddenly an incautious movement caused the rope to catch on my sleeping-bag, which I had left poised on a hold, and I spun around just in time to see it flitting down into space. I was unable to restrain a cry of rage. The loss was truly frightening. There were still great difficulties between us and the summit, and I should now be obliged to pass any further bivouacs without any shelter against the cold. The hot drink which Vaucher passed up to me helped to calm my anger.

The sky was now serene, the air biting, and the next day would be fine. This was some consolation. Over on

the final ridge of the Walker spur a light winked on,
marking the bivouac of the four we had seen earlier.
Later we learnt that they were a strong party of Germans
and Austrians who, like us, had been obliged to force
their way to the summit. To see that tiny light was like
having something to hold on to. I wanted to go on
staring at it, but the rising wind lashed my face and
numbed my body deprived of the protection of the sack.
I therefore slid my feet into the rucksack, curled up and
waited for the night to pass. Naturally there was no
question of sleeping. I was so cold that, although I tried
to think of all kinds of things, I was unable to concen-
trate on any of them. All my efforts went into controlling
my shivering body and chattering teeth, keeping the
various bits of me moving in turn, rubbing my face,
wiggling my toes, swinging my arms, massaging my
knees. The snow spume whirled up by the wind stung my
cheeks and each hour lagged longer than the last.

Next morning was Sunday. The sun was late in
appearing from behind distended clouds, pregnant with
storm in the north-east. We got under way at about
7.30. My left thumb, all swollen and black from the blow
it had received the day before, throbbed and hurt
horribly as soon as it touched anything. With a great
deal of pain I succeeded in clambering up the fixed rope
and then, using only my right hand, the remaining icy
slopes of the spider. There were now about 200 metres
between us and the top. The rock was compact, frequently overhanging and relatively clear of snow. My
thumb was now hurting as though it were cancerous, so
Vaucher took over the lead all the way to the summit.

Not only was I unable to pull up on the hand; it could not even hold the hammer, so that in order to get the pegs out I had to take tension on the rope and use my right hand instead, however inconvenient.

After a while a helicopter appeared from over the Mer de Glace and hovered backwards and forwards along the face, obviously looking for us. Unfortunately it flew too low, below our level. Presumably the pilot imagined that in view of the terrible conditions we would be retreating. Presently, however, it began to gain altitude, finally reaching our height. We could see several persons on board and waved to attract their attention, but to no avail. They looked everywhere except where we were. Next the helicopter carried out a manœuvre that left us somewhat dismayed: it dropped down to the foot of the face and inspected the glacier below the ice couloir. Clearly, not having spotted us on the face, they had decided that we were dead and were now looking for our corpses. The cheerful shouts we had bellowed at the helicopter at first now changed to curses of the most picturesque kind, accompanied with appropriate gestures. We were furious that they had failed to see us, because we knew that when they got back with their negative report those who were waiting for us would go through hours of anguish. And indeed, once the helicopter had thoroughly explored the foot of the couloir it rose rapidly towards the summit, then set off home. Thus our unique, unhoped-for chance of sending news was stupidly lost.

After this, we concentrated on nothing but the climbing. Towards midday we were swallowed up by cloud.

As we neared the crest, the humid wind encrusted our faces and clothes with white rime. By this time we were racing to escape this inferno, which had been going on for too long. Nevertheless, the climbing called for a lot of pegs. The rock was as smooth and compact as ever, and boilerplate slabs and overhangs succeeded one another unendingly, but luckily there were cracks. The whole process was further complicated by the shortness of the remaining rope, which forced us into unforeseen acrobatics, and all this in the dense cloud which limited our visibility. Finally, however, the tower up which we were climbing began to narrow and lie back until at last it became the summit. We realized almost by hazard that we had won through; it was just that there was nothing more above us.

We had won in spite of all setbacks and obstacles, but there was no time to savour our victory. The weather was still bad, night would soon be falling, and the problem of descent had to be solved immediately. It was 6.30 p.m. We started to make our way down the Italian side. But which was the Italian side? Twice I was seized with doubt. Were we starting back down the north face? Luckily the fear soon vanished. Guided partly by instinct and partly by the direction of the wind, I began to pick a way down the first rocks.

Two hundred metres below the summit darkness forced us to stop. It was snowing, and before long we were half buried. Our fourth bivouac was no less uncomfortable than the other three. In another two hours we could have reached the valley, but having put up a stiff struggle throughout the ascent, the Whymper seemed to want to avenge itself with this last surprise, which continued to complicate our descent the following morning.

Fifteen years earlier to the month, I had begun my major mountaineering by climbing the Walker spur on the same mountain. The severe profile of the Whymper spur had fascinated me then, and now the wheel had come full circle. Perhaps it was destiny that had brought me here, and destiny has a logic of its own. The buttress I had just climbed was the last unconquered bastion of the great Alpine tradition, which alas is now almost vanished.

IX

A Farewell to Mountaineering

I RETAIN ONLY a few vague recollections of early childhood, and my first really distinct memory may be said to coincide with the beginning of the Second World War. I was ten years old at the time, and from then on all the scenes and landscapes of adolescence that remain in my memory are associated with hunger. To comprehend the hunger of a boy of ten, you have to have experienced it yourself. By the time I was able to satisfy it five years later, it was time to seek work, and I already had burdens to bear. At that age time goes by slowly and every experience leaves an indelible impression in the soul. From that early stage of my existence I remember the horrible sights of the air raids; the resistance fighters, former playmates not much older than myself, with their faces kicked in and riddled with bullets; then, by the turn of the dice, the disfigured corpses of Mussolini and his ministers hanging from a petrol pump. The "Duce d'Italia", a mythical, immortal being in the hymns we were obliged to intone each morning before classes began, hung before my eyes lacerated and almost naked. One last desolate image of war brought my adolescence to a close. It was the time when the Germans were retreating out of Italy. The bridge over the Po at Cremona had been blown up, so I crossed over on a boat. The other shore was unrecognizable, littered with abandoned vehicles, pieces of artillery, armoured cars, ammunition cases and every other kind of warlike material shattered, buried and reburied innumerable times by the rain of high explosive that had been falling for weeks. Rudimentary crosses sprouted everywhere, and a foetid odour in the air bore witness to the presence of unburied corpses. I stood there alone, clutching my suitcase, then trudged 10 kilometres or so through that colossal graveyard to my parents' house. On that bank of the Po had stood the woods in which I had played, retreats of willow and poplar where the silence had been broken only by the song of crickets and the croaking of frogs.

Since that time many years have gone by and many legends in which I believed have been shattered. Nevertheless, in spite of everything, I have succeeded in developing my own philosophy and my own way of life from the lessons given by the best of all teachers, the analysis of a man's own experience. And nowadays I would not exchange my lot for that of anyone in the world. I am 43 years old, and, in general, I have not had an easy life, even in the mountains. Yet in a way my existence has been privileged because it was chosen, full, and vibrant with experience, the only reality which is really valid for me. Many people have been interested in my mountaineering achievements. Among them, some have approved of my thought and action, some have discussed and criticized them. Some have detested and others identified with me. But if my experiences form part of the complex web of human vicissitude, my successes belong to me alone, and, which is rare enough nowadays, I have paid for them in person.

It was to measure my own dimension that I scaled "impossible" mountains, impelled by the beauty of the landscape, by its challenge, and by the thirst for knowledge. But I believe that in its own way my individualism served the cause of human progress, since my undertakings incontrovertibly demonstrated man's innate powers of self-surpassment, which lie at the heart of every great achievement. I go so far as to make this declaration because in this world of arrogance modesty goes unheard.

I hold that the primary quality of a living creature is courage, in whatever form. In men I admire the courage of action, and still more the courage of renunciation.

There is a woman to whom I am linked by a true and mutual bond of love. I have no children, nor would I wish to have any in a country where a woman receives public recognition—it was in yesterday's newspaper—for giving birth twenty-six times.

Obviously, every man is a product of his time, and cannot be judged by the standards of any other. Nevertheless, it amuses me to imagine what my life might have been or be in ages before or after my own. This is a game in which the whole epic of humanity can be treated as your plaything. It suffices to select a period and given condition of life, and then to disembark in spirit from your time machine; but this never-never land will show you that in circumstances so different from your own you would neither have sought nor been able to become what you now are.

Bonatti (foreground) and Tassotti bivouacking anchored to the face during a storm on the north face of the Matterhorn.

The east face of the Grand Capucin (3,838 metres), the boldest obelisk of granite in the Alps.

There are moments in life when we feel the need to stop and draw up a personal balance-sheet of successes and disappointments; above all, there are times when we wish to check whether our aspirations are still the same, or to what extent they have changed. And because such self-appraisal can be beneficial, we need to arrive at a state of mind difficult to achieve, half-way between blind self-approbation and self-dissatisfaction, between the presumption of supposing oneself to be useful to someone and the insidious, painful apprehension of being useless. This time had now come for me, and I found myself reviewing and weighing every stage of my recent life.

In order to live in and on the mountains, in which I had believed and to which I had devoted a large part of my existence, I had considered no job beneath my dignity. Among others, naturally, I had tried being a guide, but I soon gave it up because it seemed to distort and vulgarize an ideal. I was unable to accept just anyone at the other end of my rope, nor could I translate into pecuniary terms a relationship which seemed to have no meaning unless of comradeship. Thus I was no good as a guide. Still, I needed to earn my living. Since I was passionately interested in photography, I took to giving lectures and slide-shows on the mountains and my own climbs. Spiritually speaking I was still escorting mountain-lovers up the peaks, but the relationship was less direct and thus less embarrassing. In this way I found an acceptable and satisfying substitute for "a trade", achieving success outside of pure mountaineering. Newspapers and magazines began to solicit my collaboration, making interesting proposals for journeys to distant lands. I accepted the lot, fitting it all in with my climbing life.

Thus I had come to a major crossroads.

On the one hand lay a wide world full of adventure which so far I had no more than glimpsed, but which I knew I loved; on the other the now worked-out world of mountaineering, rotten with mediocrity, incomprehension and envy. For years I had been living in a fevered atmosphere, very difficult to bear. Its unfriendliness made peace of mind hard to achieve, since the constant and tiresome need to defend myself left me nervously exhausted. I dislike martyrdom, but these were the facts. There were individuals who actually spent time looking for the tiniest personal weakness or fault, the least little crack in my defences, in order to cause me every kind of annoyance. Perhaps their motive was to prove to themselves that I was only human, which of course I am, even if my way of life is lonely and often not understood. It was not in the mountains that I was disillusioned, but in the insensitivity and denseness of certain people.

My decision was made. I would part with the mountains, but not to remain inactive in the valley. From the heights I had seen and understood other horizons. The editors of a famous magazine who had faith in me gave me an opening. Now I have other goals: I shall find my way through forests, across deserts and stormy seas towards lost islands, fabled mountains and volcanoes; I shall visit frozen lands, meet primitive people and wild animals, gaze on the remains of lost civilizations. All this I shall do in the same spirit as that in which I always climbed. Ideally, I shall take by the hand thousands of readers sensitive to the spell of adventure. My choice is most certainly not a betrayal of the mountains, but a wider expression of my love for nature as a whole, a nature ruled by the same laws and requiring the same sacrifices.

X

Matterhorn North: The Last Solo Climb

IT WAS 1965. A century earlier, on 17 July, the Englishman Edward Whymper and six companions had made the legendary first ascent of the Matterhorn, following the north-east or Hörnli ridge above Zermatt. In the course of the descent, four of the party fell to their deaths down the north face. That same glorious and tragic day Jean-Antoine Carrel, the daring Valtour-nanche guide, was also attempting the first ascent up the difficult Italian ridge, and thus lost the competition for the summit which he and the English gentleman had been carrying on for some time. Two days later, how-ever, Carrel chivalrously returned and succeeded in climbing his chosen route, thus crowning his efforts and vindicating his intuition. The era of traditional moun-taineering, of which the Matterhorn has thus always been a symbol, is often taken as dating from that memorable contest.

One by one, in different periods, the various ridges and faces of the stupendous pyramid were conquered. The north face, the most imposing and difficult of them all and thus also the most sought after, did not yield until the summer of 1931, when it was climbed by the brothers Toni and Franz Schmidt from Munich. A com-pound of all the qualities that make a north face severe,

The Dru (3,733 metres). Rising from the icy gully on the right, the Bonatti pillar is outlined against the sky.

Bonatti getting ready for his solo winter ascent of a new direct route on the north face of the Matterhorn.

it is one of the supreme Alpine test-pieces. The north faces of the Matterhorn, Eiger and Grandes Jorasses are often grouped together in an elite trio. The first ascent of the face in winter, much coveted for the demonstration of class which it would afford, was achieved in February 1963 by the remarkable Swiss climbers Hilti von Allmen and Paul Etter.

Was the splendid Matterhorn thus entirely worked out? No. On the great north face itself a direct route remained to be made. The logic of this line had been noticed as early as 1928, when Kaspar Mooser and Victor Imboden had made an unsuccessful attempt on it.

In accordance with my decision, I had not been thinking about the big climbs for many months, and had contracted with the weekly magazine *Epoca* to make a long and adventurous journey through Canada and Alaska in the spring. But somehow the mountaineering bug was still biting. With the impending anniversary of the first ascent of the Matterhorn, my old project of making a direct route up the north face using the Mooser-Imboden start came urgently back to mind. Was it the spell of a date, or was the date only a pretext? Quite apart from my project, I was burning to climb the Matterhorn and to celebrate its 100 years of history in my own way. Against my earlier word, I therefore decided to open a sort of parenthesis in my abstention from mountaineering and to close it again immediately afterwards without regret. I would go for the direct route up the north face, and since by the summer an ocean would lie between me and the Matterhorn it would just have to be done in winter.

L

There is never any shortage of volunteers to accompany anyone who is riding the crest of the wave, wherever he wants to go, whether in the world in general or in the more restricted world of mountaineering. But life taught me early that the most famous of them is not worth the most modest of genuine friends. For me, a friend is like an oasis in the human environment. It was therefore among my real friends that I sought companions for this new undertaking. Pierre Mazeaud was living in Paris, somewhat far off for regular contact, and his work as a Deputé kept him very busy. This also applied to Michel Vaucher, a mathematics teacher in Geneva. Carlo Mauri, my trusty companion on so many adventures in the Alps and farther afield, was still recovering from a ski accident, as was Roberto Gallieni. Among my close climbing friends there remained Gigi Panei and Alberto Tassotti, and I therefore decided to ask them. The first hailed from the Abruzzi, the second from the Carnic Alps; neither was young any more, but both were hard men with a morale that could stand up to anything. Like me, their love of the mountains had brought them many years ago to live at the foot of Mont Blanc—and it was at its foot that Gigi Panei was to die in an avalanche two years later.

We attacked on 10 February. Right from the beginning the face was steep, difficult, and plastered in snow. The fact that there were three of us slowed us up; the rope manœuvres took time, and the winter day was short. Nevertheless, we were a harmonious party, happy to be where we were and to be together. In our brief communications concerning rope-handling and the like my friends' wartime nicknames of "Goitone" and "Tass" recurred magically, as though time had skipped back.

We found no trace of our distant predecessors, but presumably they turned back before the part which we called "the Traverse of the Angels". It took us three days to reach the first key passage, the curving band of overhangs which imparts a sense of spiralling movement to the face. At this point, during the night, a blizzard broke over us which showed no signs of stopping.

More or less suspended from pitons, we buried ourselves in our sleeping-bags. The upper parts of our bodies were sheltered by two thin red nylon sacks that drummed and flapped alarmingly as they were lashed by snow-laden, 100 kilometre-per-hour gusts. It was a real winter storm. Twenty-four hours later, as evening fell, the hurricane reached its height. Suddenly the tent-sack bulged like a sail; Tassotti and I saw the stitches go one by one, and then all at once the whole thing exploded and became a mere rag fluttering in the wind. We desperately clutched the remnants to our faces so as to be able to breathe, and in these circumstances we passed the rest of the night, during which the barometer sank a further 15 millimetres. Clearly, the weather was going to get worse still and there was no time to be lost. As the light filtered back we began an acrobatic retreat through the storm, descending 400 metres in a continuous series of rappels.

Back at Zermatt matters reached a point where I could almost have wished to be back on the north face. Tassotti had to leave right away; he was commandant of the Army School of Mountaineering, and his leave was up. Then Panei, who was trainer of a ski team, had to start thinking about the approaching national championships and left in his turn, though with the hope that he might come back. Thus I was left alone to hold the fort until his return, though knowing his obligations I did not feel too confident about it.

The press, that terrible two-edged weapon of publicity, blazoned forth our unsuccessful attempt in great headlines. The fact that it was the centenary year, the importance of the new winter route and, why not, the failure of Bonatti, were three elements that added up to "news", and naturally the news was cultivated with great care. Thus a problem that had been neglected for forty years was revived and inflated into a race calculated to stir the blood of the most inoffensive of climbers. It was not long before this campaign produced its first effects, and the newspapers of Europe began to report that the usual Frenchman, or German, or Swiss, was making preparations to succeed where Bonatti had failed.

Thus I endured days of anxiety that reminded me somewhat of my vicissitudes following the tragedy on the central pillar of Fresnay. The weather was as unsettled as ever. As expected, Panei telephoned to say that he could not get back. "Then I'll do it alone!" I thundered into the receiver. Alone? Surely the idea was absurd in a case like this, a mere impulse of revolt. And yet, the more I thought about it, the more it began to make sense. Finally it seemed the most logical thing in the world, and I wondered why I had not thought about it in

the first place. Now I desired nothing else, and resolved
to set out the moment the weather should improve. The
changes that occur in the human mind are amazing.

There was a certain tension about my departure on
18 February. My previous attempt had caused far too
much ink to flow, and in order to avoid further comment
I had to make my preparations in absolute secrecy. I
was accompanied by Daniel Pannatier, a friend from
Zermatt, Guido Tonella from Geneva, and Mario De
Biasi, who had been my companion on the fascinating
Siberian adventure. I had asked them to come with me
to beyond the Schwarzsee in order to give prying eyes
the impression that we were going for a simple ski-tour.
When we got there I dodged behind a boulder to change
into climbing clothes and pack my sack. But at the
moment of parting, I was betrayed by emotion. I wanted
to appear calm and smiling, and all I could do was
mutter a hoarse farewell and practically run away. De
Biasi sensed my state of mind and found an excuse for
wanting to accompany me a bit farther. Above us the
Matterhorn towered ever more frowningly and blade-
sharp against a diaphanous, almost black sky. The feeling of emptiness was overpowering. I was torn between
the urge to tell my friend to turn back at once, because
the going was becoming difficult and dangerous, and my
selfish desire to have his company as long as possible.
In the event I simply let the matter slide.

Late in the afternoon we reached the Hörnli hut, but
I decided to continue on to the foot of the north face;
to pass the night between the walls of the closed-up hut
would make the feeling of loneliness more unbearable

than ever. De Biasi continued to follow me. Soon an ice-gully ahead would finally bar his way, but I still sought to spin out every minute of his company.

On the col we passed into icy shadow. The sun had already disappeared behind the mountain. What was happening to me? Why should I so fear the solitude formerly often and long desired? I continued to feel daunted and did not know how to hide it from my companion.

"I wish I were a climber so that I could come with you," said De Biasi giving me a farewell hug, and once again I did not know how to reply. There was a lump in my throat. Fearing to see him going away, I did not even have the courage to look back. Yet it was late, and a long and difficult descent to the valley lay before him. It was logical that he should go. An awkward movement across a crevasse forced me to turn around. De Biasi was still there. Only then did my voice come back to me.

"It'll be all right!" I called.

"Yes, Walter," he replied, and disappeared beyond the ridge.

I was bewildered with emotion and the total silence of the mountains. The sun was setting, and all around me lay an extinct, empty world, hostile to man and every form of life. Everything in this world, the rock, the ice, the snow, the mountain itself, was held in suspense be-tween reality and imagination. In order not to be afraid I forced myself to think of nothing at all, making my way towards the foot of the face like an automaton. There was a big sérac to surmount, and on the flatter ground above I found here and there our footprints from the earlier attempt, case-hardened by the wind. The discovery brought me neither comfort nor relief.

Darkness caught me as I was hacking out a platform on the glacier on which I could curl up in my sleeping-bag. "If the weather would turn bad I could go back down out of here in the morning," I thought, and then: "Supposing I did it anyway, right now?" At that moment lights began to shine up from the valley. They were turning on the lamps in Zermatt. Their rays carried swarms of thoughts up to me, but all came back to the same point: should I retreat or not? Yet, for no reason I can explain, I remained where I was. The whole night went by without sleep coming to calm my agitation. My eyes were unwilling to quit the black shadow of the mountain wall impending above me.

At dawn the cold became unbearable, and as I slid out of my sleeping-bag I felt clumsy and numb. When at last I was ready to move I stood for a few moments undecided whether to continue upwards or to retreat to Zermatt. As I took the first step towards the face I was aware that I was pitting myself against a self-imposed test of courage.

The wall was hostile right from the start. It was necessary to place a piton for security, and as I groped around in the sack for one I found a pair of sealskins.* How they had got there I had no idea, but anyway they represented useless weight, and much against my will I had to throw them away down the slope. Zizì seemed to smile at this unexpected joke. Zizì was a tiny teddy-bear that Pannatier's smallest son had given me as a mascot

---

* *Translator's note:* Clipped under skis for walking uphill. Nowadays made of plush, they retain the originally accurate name.

for this adventure. Since setting out the day before I had been carrying it attached to my sack, and already I had grown fond of it.

From now on the climbing absorbed all my attention, a veritable spiritual liberation. The first day slipped by quickly and virtually without incident. So intent was I that I did not even find time to eat. My method was as follows: I would attach the sack to a piton just as though it were a companion, then climb for the full length of the 40 metre rope, which I would attach to another piton. Next I would go down to the sack, take it on my shoulders and climb back up, taking out any pitons on the way. Time and effort could no longer be counted. To reach the summit, I should in effect have to climb the whole north face twice and descend it once.

The second night caught me on the open face, still 15 metres from the sole ledge on which there was room to sit down. I forced the pitch in darkness and reached the ledge just in time to spot the prearranged light signal from De Biasi in the valley, to which I replied. The wind gusted brutally across the crags. Though racked with thirst I could not summon up the energy to melt snow for a drink, but simply pulled the bivouac sack over me. A merry-go-round of images, some clear and some vague, passed through my mind . . . the Siberian *iurte* in far-off Yakutia, my father, the sea at San Fruttuoso, roses in the garden of one of my friends, Inspector Maigret drinking a tankard of beer, the faces of people I loved. Again a feeling of infinite loneliness overwhelmed me.

As the night went on the sky began to cloud over. It

looked as though another sudden change of weather were on the way. When I consulted the barometer, however, the needle was steady at a high figure. According to the instrument there was nothing to worry about, though my instinct was all for instant retreat in order to save myself from hours in another storm. On my return I was to learn that during the course of that night five centimetres of snow had fallen on the south face of the Matterhorn. Dawn dispersed the clouds and the weather turned splendid again.

It was almost noon as I began the Traverse of the Angels. The rock was extremely smooth and compact, making it difficult to find anywhere to place pitons. Those I did succeed in placing were none too sound. The angle was such that the climbing was almost acrobatic, and I had to take extreme care. In addition, the traverse was plastered with a layer of unstable snow which had to be cleared away at each movement. If Panei had only been less conscientious about taking out the pegs, it would have saved me a lot of trouble now. In all, there are 120 metres of traverse from right to left over steep, icy, treacherous slabs, and these took me the rest of the day. I advanced warily, hammered in a few pitons which had more psychological than real value, then returned, shouldered my sack which seemed to grow heavier as I got more tired, and finally moved up again to the top of the pitch taking out the pitons as I went. I should have stopped to eat, but the thought hardly crossed my mind. Throughout the whole day I only sucked a few lumps of sugar.

Occasionally aeroplanes flew around the face. Clearly

they were looking for me, and I wondered if they had picked me out. They climbed and dived in wide spirals like birds of prey borne on the wind, dark in the cold shadow of the face or small and sparkling in the sunlight when they banked away.

Towards evening I reached the bivouac place where the storm had blocked the three of us for two nights and a day. On the narrow ledge lay over a dozen pitons and a bag of food we had left behind. It had been Panei's job to take out the pitons, and so scrupulous had he been that in two days' climbing I had so far found only one. I anchored myself securely, balanced the cooker on my knees, and brewed a hot drink. While doing this I caught myself talking aloud to my two companions who were not there.

As happened every evening when the action was over, a thousand thoughts began to assail me, and I was overwhelmed with the magnitude of my undertaking. Ahead of me now, beyond the overhangs just above my head, lay the unknown and the virtual certainty of not being able to retreat on account of the curious twisting form of the overhangs, which would force me to make complicated pendulum rappels swinging clear in space. It was strange to think that there below me, growing more distant every day, life was going on, perhaps easy and alluring to one who like me was now suspended between heaven and earth, yet so banal and disappointing that a man would climb up here in order to escape it. But for all that, the solitude was fearful and inhuman. I asked myself if I had not overstepped the limits of prudence, and whether in my pride I had not challenged the fates.

Perhaps words like "prudence" and "fate" have no value except in relation to what we are, and do not bear the same countenance for us all. If this were so, prudence for me would be to attack the north face of the Matterhorn, and fate to reach the summit. From here on there could be no other way.

I looked at my watch: it was just before 7.30 p.m., the time we had arranged to exchange signals. Zermatt was all lit up as usual, but those were not the lights I was waiting for. This evening I had important news to communicate to my friend in the valley: I had decided to go on to the summit. Half an hour later, when I finally picked out De Biasi's signal, I replied with a white flare to draw his attention, followed by a green one to show that I was continuing. Had I intended to retreat I was to have fired a red flare, and since this was now useless I threw it away.

While I was sorting out the bivouac things my peg hammer fell off the ledge. Luckily I had a spare, or I would have been well and truly stuck. The uncomfortable position in which I was jammed obstructed my circulation. I could feel an ominous chill in my feet, so I kicked them around to bring them back to warmth. So it went on all night, between sleep and waking.

As I started up the overhangs in the early morning the sack seemed so heavy that immediately after the difficulties I resolved to take a decisive step. I could not go on like this. I therefore opened the sack and started eliminating whatever did not seem indispensable. First a lump of cheese went flying into space, then two gas canisters, followed by a volley of jam, bacon, biscuits, dried meat, powdered soup, sugar and condensed milk. It was a pity that I could not leave them somewhere in a hollow for the benefit of someone else, but the trouble was that there were no hollows. The packages fell with dull thuds that were soon swallowed up in the void. My daily output of calories must have been at least 10,000, but it was all I could do to swallow 500.

The barrier of overhangs that cut off any hope of retreat now lay below me. There was therefore no choice but to reach the summit. As though hypnotized, I climbed on almost automatically towards a second vertical wall. My mind, numbed with loneliness and cold, seemed unable to retain ideas; I had to seize them as they slid away and put them forcibly back in place, or I would have run the risk of falling at any moment. I therefore stopped and shook myself, willing my brain into clarity.

Beyond the wall lay a snare in the form of a wide zone of smooth, ice-glazed rock, that seemed to bar the route entirely. It was now 4 o'clock in the afternoon, so that there remained some two more hours of daylight. As I surveyed the snare, I thought I could see a good bivouac spot beyond it on the right. The sky was translucent, the colour of glazed lead; the air lugubrious, of a marble-like quality; the cold such as you would imagine in interstellar space; the silence paralyzing. The only sounds were the rustling of my anorak in the wind and the faint abrasive drifting of snowdust across the rocks. On all sides there remained no single thing to recall humanity. I looked at Zizì, the tiny teddy-bear, who never stopped smiling with his great yellow glass eyes.

"What do you think, Zizì, shall we try to reach that ledge up there?"

Instinctively I caressed him, and for the first time I noticed that my hands were cracked and bleeding with the cold. So far I had only been able to keep on my gloves for short stretches.

I was now reaching the limits of the possible and felt so outside the world that when I thought of something beautiful and human I was wrung with emotion. More coated in ice than ever, the face had lost every vestige of form and appeared to me like the hollow of a colossal seashell with myself in the centre, trying to climb up. When I raised my eyes I could not see the summit, when I looked down Zermatt was hidden from view. Dislodged by the wind, a few stones shot whirring down into space. By an association of ideas this made me think of the accident 100 years earlier. That avalanche of bodies in 1865 must have passed very close to where I stood. It was a macabre vision. I wanted to get out of this place as soon as possible.

Night fell. I was tired, tired to death. My mouth was burning with thirst and my saliva had a bitter taste. I still do not really know how I found somewhere to bivouac.

Darkness, wind, frost, and a surfeit of scheming, searching, fighting with the daylight.

Once again, perched on a ledge a foot wide which I had cleared of ice, my back against the rock and my feet dangling in space, held in place by two loops of rope, one around my chest and the other around my knees, I was unable to sleep even for a moment.

Morning was slow in coming. It was now 6.30 a.m. on Monday, 22 February. My fourth bivouac was coming to an end; perhaps it would be the last. The little thermometer hanging on my anorak indicated −30°C. My face had grown a fringe of icicles that burned the skin. Inside the tent-sack my hands had been spasmodically grasping the torch for at least half an hour as I waited to reply to De Biasi's light signal. In a barn far down in the valley he too would be waiting. Now it was only a few minutes before the appointed time. There was a full moon, but the shadow of the mountain lay over the place from which he would signal. A single thought possessed me: to see the light and to reply. I would send three or four slow flashes, then the same number of quick ones to tell him that all was well and that I had survived the night and was ready to fight on.

There it was at last. The tiny point of light seemed even smaller than it had the morning before, perhaps because I was higher up the face. It looked like the point of a red-hot needle piercing the blackness. Maybe this would be the last time I should see it; with a bit of luck I should reach the summit today. The flashes were given slowly. There were four of them. I drew my hand out of the sack and replied at the same rate. I had been seen: now it was time for the quick flashes. By contrast with the others, these seemed as lively and full of feeling as words. I replied equally hurriedly, as though calling out loud. That small light from my friend 2,000 metres below in the valley was the only human contact that had accompanied me for three days and nights.

The sky was growing grey. The lights of Zermatt

vanished one by one in the pallor of dawn. Then everything was imbued with one immense, boundless, weight-
less blue. Before that infinity I lingered on, thirsty to
absorb the universe. The well-known saying "the centre
is everywhere, the circumference nowhere" found its
perfect expression before my eyes.

Drunken with silence and freed from the fetters of
thought and action, my spirit exulted, giving a meaning
to my adventure. A hundred years earlier, Whymper
had arrived at Zermatt in a diligence, and in order to
climb this mountain had organized an expedition with
guides and porters, as is still done in the Andes and
Himalayas. Now an unpiloted spaceship was about to
be launched towards the moon to gather and transmit
information about the lunar surface, where man would
soon tread. A hundred years of history and vertiginous
technical progress divided these two enterprises; and yet
I, a man of my time, still felt the need to return to the
spirit of the ancient heroes, the pattern of David and
Goliath. I felt certain that my small green light would
have been received down there as a message, touching
hearts and making them feel more human.

The start of the day's climbing was violent. Above my
head stretched 30 metres of overhanging, loose rock that
had to be climbed. Judging from the number of aircraft
circling around, the summit could not be too far away, so
I sought to lighten the sack again in order to move
faster. I therefore chucked away more food, a couple of
étriers and a number of pitons. I was tempted to get rid
of my crash-helmet too, but after a moment's hesitation
I squeezed it against me. The trusty old helmet had been

my companion on all my hardest climbs of the last four years. I stroked the scratches in its surface as though they had been wounds: they corresponded to as many stones falling from the slopes of Mont Blanc, the Andes and many other ranges. Finally I hung it on the sack beside the teddy-bear and started to climb.

Towards midday I thought I heard the sound of cries between the gusts of wind. A few minutes later they were repeated. Without any doubt, there was someone above me. But where? On the summit or one of the two flanking ridges? So I yelled back: "Who are you? Where are you?" From their replies I was able to orientate myself with regard to the summit, since within my field of vision there was nothing but shapeless rocks. Outlined against the ice-blue sky, the Matterhorn seemed to have no summit at all. Presently the voices faded out on the wind, and everything was as before. On my return I was deeply moved to learn that the voices had belonged to three Breuil guides who had ascended by the ordinary route in order to re-erect in my honour the iron cross that had been blown over by a winter gale.

I was alone again with my weariness. The efforts of the last few days and the increasingly rarefied air made the weight of the sack seem more and more intolerable, and I had a vision of myself as a mythical character doomed for his sins to go on climbing forever. It was not until nearly 3 o'clock in the afternoon, when I was no more than 50 metres from the top, that the cross suddenly appeared shining above me, incandescent in the sunlight that fell on it out of the south. I stood there dazzled, thinking of the haloes of the saints. Even the

Bonatti on the summit of the Matterhorn, 3 p.m. on 22 February 1965.

Bonatti's new direct route on the north face of the Matterhorn, climbed alone and in winter.

pilots of the aeroplanes that had been deafening me seemed to feel the solemnity of the moment. Perhaps out of sensitivity, they circled away and let me climb the last few metres alone and in stillness. As though under a spell I stretched up my arms to the cross and embraced it, my knees buckled and I wept.

XI

The Weight of a Medal

THE NEW CENTENARY route up the north face of the
Matterhorn was my farewell to extreme mountaineering.
It is a fact that any undertaking primarily represents an
affirmation of the personality that has conceived and
carried it out, but this one was intended as a token of
love towards the mountains, of admiration for the great
Whymper, of my emotion at the price paid in blood by
his four companions, and as a homage to the tenacity
and unconquerable will of Jean-Antoine Carrel. I
wanted it to be not so much a personal conquest as a
victory of the human spirit, the affirmation of an ethic
and a morality. For me, these values constitute its
essential meaning.

In spite of this, my ascent was described as "setting
three records in inhumanity: direct, alone and in
winter". One journalist commented that this single
climb "had written on the mountain a historical advance
that normally required several stages, different men and
several decades". Some, such as the author Dino Buzzati
and the solitary navigator Sir Francis Chichester, described it as "exceptional", because "such crazy adventures call not so much for muscular strength or
technical skill as for force of character and moral resources". A well-known mountain-climber, by contrast,

wanted to play down the importance of the climb and spoke of the need to "reassess the undertaking". At the proposal of the Minister for Home Affairs, the President of Italy awarded me the gold medal for civil valour "for an epic undertaking which excited the wonder and admiration of the whole world and the pride of our native land", in which he discerned "a symbol of the superiority of the spirit of man over material forces".

For months following this award the correspondence columns of the Italian press were full of letters and replies in which one might read, for example: "President Saragat did well to decorate Bonatti publicly so as to emphasize the high moral significance of his act." This was written by signor F.V., but signora M.B. of San Lorenzo della Costa did not agree with him, defining my climb as "useless, absurd, conceited and foolhardy", and protesting "Civil valour? Did Bonatti scale the Matterhorn to rescue a mountaineer in distress?" To this signor Ferr. replied: "Does Bonatti deserve an award? It seems obvious to me that he does. Would a sporting medal be enough? I would say not. . . . If we exclude sporting distinction as being too limited and nowadays too dubious, and since this is not a case of military bravery, then clearly the medal for civil valour is the right one. This is not specifically reserved for the saving of life, but may be given for an individual act of bravery such as, for example, those of spacemen." After noting that "poetry is useless too, and so is love unless directed specifically to the propagation of the species", signor Ferr. continued: "In fact I doubt if the ascent was useless, if only on account of its spiritual meaning and

the orientation to which it points. During the time that
Bonatti was on the mountain a mother killed herself
and her children; a father destroyed his entire family;
the 'ultima raffica' was given away by the signing of
rubber cheques; the health scandal was debated; people
presented false income-tax returns, robbed, blasphemed
and fornicated; a gang of bandits . . . and so on. Nevertheless, one man acted in quite a different way, uselessly,
absurdly, with foolhardiness, and—the word fits—
poetically. How could his deeds fail to comfort us?"

Yet the old, inevitable question was brought up again,
this time by signor Rocco Mariani who began his letter
with it: "What use are such feats?" According to signor
Gaetano Gattinara: "To be for or against Bonatti's
undertaking is equivalent to being for enlightenment or
obscurantism, and every man has the right and the duty
to choose for himself." Farther on he added: "His
achievement is anything but useless, and even if it were
so, it is after all this element of uselessness which endows
life with poetry and beauty. A flower in a living-room
serves no useful purpose; but it is precisely its lack of any
practical utility which renders it beautiful."

The speleologist Pietro Zuccato was of a completely
different opinion. He declared himself perplexed by my
decoration. "If the criterion for such an award is, to go
back to the wording, to have upheld the name and
prestige of a country," he said, "then the winners in the
Olympic Games should have been similarly decorated . . .
not to mention champions in all popular sports or those
who, without publicity or thought of personal advantage,
face danger for their personal pleasure and to make a

contribution to science. Such a distribution of honours would be more equitable." The newspaper commented: "A good many people have maintained, as is your opinion and ours, that the proper medal to have awarded for this solo ascent would have been the gold medal for athletic achievement." It concluded: "In the initial enthusiasm aroused by Bonatti's exceptional feat and its impact in foreign countries, the authorities probably forgot about the existence of the gold medal for athletic achievement."

There followed a great deal of further correspondence for and against my climb and my medal, but it was the last in chronological order that really caused dismay. It ran as follows:

"There is a wrong that should be set right. . . . Is it right and moral that the gold medal for civil valour or civil merit should be awarded to Walter Bonatti? . . . The mountaineer, in a spirit of sportsmanship, should therefore return the decoration received."

The reader may wonder why I should wish to quote these opinions, together with all the criticisms of my activities which I have mentioned in earlier chapters. It gives me no pleasure to speak of such things, but pain sometimes needs an outlet. One of my reasons has been that if I explain some of the "marginal" aspects of my story it is more likely to be understood. For better or worse, our actions are in the last resort never entirely our own, but are always subject to external influences. Persons and facts, circumstances and judgements, have often been motives and incentives to me in my ventures. Thus I am in debt to others at least to the extent that my deeds belong to them.

Bonatti the man has now ceased to be Bonatti the climber. I shall shortly be leaving for Alaska, an adventurous journey through a vast, still unspoiled landscape, the essence of which can worthily succeed the "north faces". So I want to finish here, with this last vision of the Matterhorn. I imagine them all, the supporters and the detractors, debating the man, the scene, the challenge, the courage, the significance, the pride, the comparable cases, the soul, infinity, conquest, in short the whole range of subjects which all too often begin and end with the usual unfruitful "why?" or give rise to the empty question "Was it worth it?" Physically, as we all know, one man is worth as much as another. It is the psychological differences which really differentiate us and give the measure of a human being. To know who we are and what we ought to do should be everybody's first duty, but how many really seek the truth? How many are willing without any casuistry to assume the responsibility of a choice?

No, I am not a sham, a self-fabricated image. I exist materially, just as I am, in this factual world which we all inhabit. My way of living has never been intended to provoke anybody, as has often been suggested, but rather to bring comfort. If some people find it an affront to the conformism of our age, that may indeed be its justification.

I would like to say a special word of farewell to climbers, and in particular to those who are dedicated to competition and to the development of the sport.

Obviously, there is more to mountaineering than its extreme expression in surpassment and affirmation, but it remains true that this is one very important side of it. Anyone who hopes to push back the limits of human possibility still further—naturally I speak in terms of the classical tradition—cannot be satisfied with copying what has been done already. Any repetition, though a praiseworthy thing in itself, cannot by definition improve on what has already been achieved.

Among climbers there is one who has set himself up, or who has at least allowed himself to be set up, as my judge. It would be an honour and a source of pride for me if this person would—if he can—take up the torch I left on the Matterhorn and carry it farther along the same road. Only thus will he avoid letting down himself, me, and a glorious past.

The distance that I myself was able to travel along this road of tradition is described in these pages. In order to go any farther (perhaps this sounds immodest, but if I am to be clear I must be objective) I myself would be obliged to add a new factor, namely very high altitude. My next step would thus be to extend to the Himalaya what I have done in the Alps, in other words to apply Alpine techniques at 8,000 metres. Perhaps I would begin by climbing one of the giants without oxygen or fixed camps, simply making do with bivouacs. Then I would try solo ascents, solo winter ascents, and finally solo winter ascents by the most difficult unclimbed routes. Naturally, all this is a daring vision, since man's unaided force will never be great enough to achieve it. Still, it should be noted how much "raw material" the mountains still hold in reserve for traditional mountaineering; enough for any amount of progress, enough to satisfy the most exacting of mountaineers who wishes to apply only his personal, human resources. It is true that even the most accessible of these goals now seems terrifying and incredible, precisely because it still lies before us; but I do not think that the east face of the Grand Capucin, the bivouac without shelter in the storm at over 8,000 metres on K 2 or the solo first ascent of the south-west pillar of the Dru seemed any more probable before I made them a reality.

Undeniably, the enormous lure of the impossible and the unknown has always inspired men to adventure, in the mountains as elsewhere. Yet it is obvious that the impossible of today may no longer be that of tomorrow, and that what is insuperable for one man may not be so for another, more gifted and better prepared. Clearly, however, if the impossible is to maintain its fascination it must be overcome and not simply abolished. It should not be forgotten that the value of the high mountains is that of the men who measure themselves against them: otherwise they are no more than heaps of stone.

Index

Index